George Herbert Curteis

The Scientific Obstacles to Christian Belief

George Herbert Curteis

The Scientific Obstacles to Christian Belief

ISBN/EAN: 9783337417062

Printed in Europe, USA, Canada, Australia, Japan

Cover: Foto ©Lupo / pixelio.de

More available books at **www.hansebooks.com**

THE SCIENTIFIC OBSTACLES TO CHRISTIAN BELIEF.

BOYLE LECTURES, 1884.

BY

GEORGE HERBERT CURTEIS, M.A.,

CANON RESIDENTIARY OF LICHFIELD CATHEDRAL;
EXAMINING CHAPLAIN TO THE BISHOP OF LICHFIELD;
PROFESSOR OF NEW TESTAMENT EXEGESIS IN KING'S COLLEGE, LONDON.

London:
MACMILLAN AND CO.
1885.

The Right of Translation and Reproduction is Reserved.

LONDON:
R. CLAY, SONS, AND TAYLOR,
BREAD STREET HILL, E.C.

PREFACE.

Extract from a Codicil to the Last Will and Testament of the HON. ROBERT BOYLE, ESQ., *dated July* 28, 1691.

"WHEREAS I have an intention to settle in my lifetime the sum of Fifty Pounds per annum for ever, or at least for a considerable number of years, to be for an annual salary for some learned Divine or Preaching Minister, from time to time to be elected and resident within the city of London or circuit of the Bills of Mortality, who shall be enjoined to perform the offices following, viz.—To preach Eight Sermons in the year, for Proving the Christian Religion against notorious Infidels, viz., Atheists, Theists, Pagans, Jews, and Mahometans, not descending lower to any controversies that are among Christians themselves : these Lectures to be on the first Monday of the respective months of January, February, March, April, May, September, October, November, in such church as my trustees herein named shall from time to time appoint;[1] to be assisting to all Companies, and encouraging of them in any undertaking for Propagating the Christian Religion in foreign parts; to be ready to satisfy such real scruples as any may have concerning these matters, and to answer such new objections and difficulties as may be started, to which good answers have not yet been made. . . . I will that after my death Sir John Rotherham, Sergeant-at-Law, Sir Henry Ashurst, of London, Knight and Baronet, Thomas Tennison, Doctor in

[1] The Boyle Lectures are now preached in the Chapel Royal, Whitehall, on some of the Sundays following Easter Day, in the afternoon.

Divinity, and John Evelyn, sen., Esq., and the survivors or survivor of them, and such person or persons as the survivor of them shall appoint to succeed in the following trust, shall have the election and nomination of such Lecturer, and also shall and may constitute and appoint him for any term not exceeding three years, and at the end of such term shall make a new election and appointment of the same or any other learned Minister of the Gospel, residing within the city of London or extent of the Bills of Mortality, at their discretions."

THE rapid spread of unbelief in England during the last ten years has struck every observer. But its causes have been very superficially investigated. Christians have been in too great a hurry to defend what was so justly dear to their own hearts. And the all-important question has therefore been deferred, which ought to have stood first in their deliberations for defence, viz., *What precisely are, at the present day, the obstacles to Christian belief?* Until that question has been faced and answered, apologists are in danger of striking quite wide of the mark, and of simply "beating the air." No doubt even such ill-directed energy has its value. It displays to all beholders the extreme preciousness of the Gospel to those who have the privilege of retaining their faith; and it confirms the assurance and animates the courage of the great mass of implicit believers.

What such hasty and random strategy, however, does *not* do is to maintain the cause of Christ against outside attacks, and to convince unbelievers. For that purpose quite another sort of strategy is needful. The apologist must calmly "sit down first and count the cost." In other words, he must bravely face the full perils of the situation; he must not under-estimate the forces which his adversary is able to bring into the field; he must intuitively enter into the opponent's views, appropriate and (as it were) sympathise with them, and divine beforehand what is likely to be advanced in maintaining them. Above all, the Christian leader—if he is to win, not merely a skirmish, or even a battle, but the whole campaign—must "count the cost" in another sense. He must know what to surrender. It is merely brutal and useless strategy to defend everything without discrimination. In every age some points become of less vital importance than they were before; some breastworks are found to be incompetent to resist improved methods of attack; and some outlying defences, to every eye but that of their passionate defender, have manifestly become worse than useless, mere traps for impounding and wasting the force urgently required elsewhere, mere gratuitous invitations to the foe to effect a lodgment and to proclaim a victory, if not actually to gain one.

For instance, it should be clearly understood by all who would defend the Christian faith in England, that here (at least) no *scorn* is felt for that faith. The extraordinary blessing which divine Providence has accorded to this country in her possession of a reformed and ever-reforming, yet at the same time catholic and historical and national, Church has secured us against that danger. Had the Church of England presented, at this moment, the aspect either of a powerful, but unreformed, corporation—or had she, on the other hand, been reformed indeed, but frittered into innumerable and powerless fragments, had she lost her catholic organisation, or forfeited her claim to be the old historic Church of the nation—in either case the defence of Christianity would have been greatly compromised. Contempt would have been felt and expressed for an organism which had grown too ossified and senile to bear the touch of reform; and indifference would be expressed for a spiritual discipline which failed to command the allegiance, or to stir the enthusiasm, even of its own professed adherents. Surrounded, however, as she now is, by a host of minor voluntary societies, which act as safety-valves against over-government within, and provide a happy refuge without for every serious discontent, the Church of England has thus far amply justified her privileged position in this country, and has—by the almost universal admission of her foes—formed the main bulwark of modern Christendom against unbelief.

To this body, then, above all others, seems now committed by divine Providence, the task of making head against the advancing inroads of nineteenth century unbelief. It is a many-sided body. It offers "facets" (as it were) corresponding to many points of the mental compass. But especially its three great schools of opinion—the so-called High, Low, and Broad parties—present fronts of sympathy and attraction for the three main types of, at least Anglo-Saxon, mankind. In the HIGH CHURCH school the imaginative element predominates; and in the touching beauty of its ritual and the lovely tranquillity and peaceable self-subordination that reign there, thousands of devout souls have found a quiet framework for their religious lives, and a soothing remedy against that morbid excitement which too often unsettles and deranges minds of the devotional type. Indeed, much more than this may now be said in thankful recognition of what the so-called Catholic Revival in the Church of England has done for English Christianity. There are hundreds of intellectual men, and men of high scientific or literary acquirements, to whom *the mental liberty accorded by a ritual presentment of religious ideas* has been salvation and peace. These men are, in every sense, the cream of English society. They are the best of England's sons. To lose them, to make religion difficult and unacceptable to them, to impose upon them elaborate theological burdens, and insist on their accepting the Gospel in (what may perhaps be called) its pulpit form, or not accepting it at all—this would be gross folly and consummate treason to Christ. For the Gospel is far more than its form of presentment, as even the Apostles found out, when they were divinely led to break with the Jewish system in which it had been originally inshrined. The framework of Christianity therefore became from that time forward more elastic, and freedom of mental movement within it grew more assured as all sorts and conditions of men came in. And the great Apostle who first carried the Church boldly into Europe, and bowed the Greek mind beneath the gentle yoke of Christ, gloried in that elasticity and freedom; he joyfully became "all things to all men," and exultingly proclaimed to the Gentile world, "Stand fast in the liberty wherewith Christ hath made you free!"

But not even in his time, when the leaven of the Gospel was seizing and permeating with its marvellous potency Hellenic philosophy and Roman statecraft, was this freedom so essential as it is now. For in *physical science* a really new world of thought has of late years been discovered; and so the very opening which Alexander sighed for in vain, "a new world to conquer," has been providentially made ready for a general advance of the whole forces of the Church. And in *literature*, too, such revelations have lately been made, by procuring for linguistic and historical study the various sacred books of the far east, by compelling the long silent hieroglyphics of Egypt to give up their secret, and by disinterring from their dusty graves the tablet libraries of the Assyrian kings that a summons to break with merely classical and mediæval formulæ of thinking seems as clearly in the air as when St. Paul proclaimed emancipation from the Jewish law.

Not that any real breach of continuity is either necessary or possible. And here the evangelical, or so-called Low Church, party may—if they will only rise to their golden opportunity—do most precious service to their Master's cause. For to them, above all men, St. Augustine's motto seems peculiarly to belong:—"Transeunt nubes, cœlum manet,"—"Let God be true, though every man be a liar; traditions, rituals, all the mechanism and paraphernalia of divine things, may easily change and pass away, provided only the truth they all express and embody remains intact." And so this school hold themselves in trust with the naked spiritual verities, the ideals, the essential heart-transforming truths, which the traditional school has mainly charged itself with the task of clothing in elaborate ceremonial and symbol. And if the modern man desires above all things to retain his grasp of Christian ideals, while he simply helps himself, as he was meant to do, by ecclesiastical art and sees through it such higher and spiritual truth as his soul may be able, from time to time, to assimilate, surely such a free use of ceremony and sacrament is precisely what a Low Churchman should approve. But he must have patience and tolerance for what seem to him doctrinal immaturities and imperfections. And he should remember that, as with ritual forms of expression, so with dogmatic and verbal formulæ of divine truth, " the clouds pass over, but the blue sky remains behind."

And as for the third school, the (so-called) BROAD CHURCH party in our English Christendom, the representative of the more intellectual side of religious life, it is quite obvious that this is the most natural of all allies for men of science and refinement who also desire to be Christians. Along this " facet" of the Church reason is ever busy, and is ever claiming fellow-workers in the difficult task of penetrating—so far as God shall empower the human mind to do so—the mysteries of God with the light of clear intelligence. And as Science, for her part, is doing precisely the same with the dark mysteries of nature, it seems that complete harmony should here exist; and that this school is especially charged to clothe with ever new interest for intellectual men the varied problems which theology presents. For we need not fear, in the name of God, any truth whatever, and should endeavour to tinge with spiritual consecration the brave and patient toil of workers in every branch of human endeavour.

But for all schools alike, and for every religious man who would "serve his own generation by the will of God," one maxim is nowadays essential, one motto should be for ever present in the mind. It is the same as that stirring call of the Catholic Church of Christ in all ages, from the very beginning, "Sursum corda!" Lift up your hearts! Raise up your thoughts to higher planes of thinking than you have ever yet habitually lived in! It is by the simple process of taking higher, grander, less unworthy, more cosmic, more elevated, views of God and of divine things, that a thousand modern difficulties about these baffling subjects are resolved and vanish of themselves— as vapour is absorbed into dry air, or as childish perplexities disappear in mature life. If Englishmen and Englishwomen could only be persuaded firmly to believe that religion demands the exercise of our very highest powers—intellectual, imaginative, and moral—they surely would, without "evil surmisings" or jealous party enmities, warmly welcome every fellow-worker in this difficult but captivating department of mental labour. And then a possible future might open before this country which it is entrancing to contemplate. She might, with her grand historical

Church and her multitude of acute and strenuous workers in every department of mental labour, easily become a blessing to universal Christendom: and to her own sons, whether at home or in the colonies or in foreign kindred states, England might be—as she is already on the way to be—a *Terra Sancta*, a sort of Holy Land, a mother land whence influences far better, more noble, more free, than any which mediæval Europe drew from Rome, might constantly radiate around. Her soil is crowded with the most beautiful and interesting relics of bygone centuries; nowhere can the Christian life of the past be better studied than here; in no country and in no Church are old institutions, old service-books, old ceremonies, old buildings, to be seen as they are in England—alive not dead, reformed not petrified, adapted to and nourishing an active Christian faith of a modern kind, and not a Christianity artificially preserved from decay by exclusion of the fresh wholesome air and by precautions worthy of Egyptian Pharaohs, whose highest ambition was gratified when their dead bodies were made impervious to all change.

In this connection, I cannot refrain from quoting the language of an American writer on

England, which appeared not long ago in a New York magazine. "Nature with us [in the United States] is a harsh, unloving stepmother. She has the continental swing and stride and the continental indifference. The dominant impression of the English landscape is repose. Never was such a restful land to the eye—especially to the American eye, satiated with the mingled splendour and squalor of his own landscape, its violent contrasts, and general spirit of unrest. England is the old homestead. It is grandfather's and grandmother's land. It is the seat of the dominant race. The American feels 'at home' there." (*The Century*, November, 1883.) The same feeling is constantly expressed by visitors to our sacred ancestral land, both American and colonial. May nothing be done to impair it! May everything be done to strengthen and to elevate it! And, still more, may every effort be made to consecrate it to highest Christian uses; and so to make it, in the most telling and permanent way of all, a spirit of unity and a "bond of peace."

CONTENTS.

LECTURE I.

HISTORICAL INTRODUCTION.

Foundations of Christian belief rudely shaken nowadays.—Even women affected by unbelief.—Christendom should arouse itself to grapple with the problem.—What are the modern obstacles to belief?—First question a historical one.—Is it from fault of our own, or by the ordinary laws of intellectual progression?—Our planet has swept into new environments.—Old evidences have lost their value.—Each generation has its own difficulties to encounter.—Gnosticism the first wave of intellectual difficulty.—Another wave after a thousand years.—Church accepted the aids of heathen logic and metaphysics but rejected crude theories of physical science.—A third wave five hundred years later.—Deism and other forms of unbelief.—Christendom riven into numberless divisions.—And now, another wave-crest of unbelief towers above our modern controversies.—Darwin's honoured name.—His disciples outstrip their master.—Nature-Worship proposed by some.—The law of recurring unbelief.—Intellect and imagination need to be well balanced.—Faith is the common ground for all.
Pages 1—23.

LECTURE II.

GOD.

Intellect and imagination two factors working together.—How controversies arise.—Contrast, in foreign cities, of fanaticism and atheism.—Happy the nations that soften the asperities of conflict.—Duty of conciliation on both sides.—Work of intellect analytical and discriminative.—Work of imagination to make things human.—Anthropomorphism therefore necessary.—Worship of mere nature impossible; or of mere humanity.—Evil inexplicable on any theory.—Materialism a real obstacle.—But matter and force two different things.—Theism, not Atheism, satisfies the human mind.—Human knowledge only relative.—Intellect, imagination and conscience, triple functions of the mind.—Faith a prime necessity.—Combining unknown power, unfathomable wisdom, and firm will, into a superior unity, we so worship God.—Impossible to believe in an evil power guiding the universe.—The cosmic force not unconscious.—The Christian conception of a personal God rational and satisfactory. . . . . *Pages* 24—50.

LECTURE III.

CREATION.

Christian doctrine that God created and sustains nature.—Mind antecedent to matter.—Simple picture-language of Genesis justified.—The "carpenter theory of creation" a man of straw.—"Evolution" supplements creation, does not contradict it.—Primal creative "word" expanded into a majestic stream of physical legislation.—By the logos, or intelligible reason of God all things were made.—Fate, an irrational conception.—Cosmic forces awful, but not fateful.—The power that governs the universe is not fate, but a living God.—Clue furnished by our own will.—

"Chance" an irrational idea.—Letters thrown on floor could never arrange themselves into a play of Shakspeare.—And impossible to grant infinite time.—Earth not long ago a mass of molten lava.—Theory of creation, supplemented by "evolution" is, after all, the most satisfactory.
Pages 51—67.

LECTURE IV.

MIRACLE.

Scientific men turn away from miracle with dislike.—Fuller liberty should be accorded than in times gone by.—Timely deference and breadth of view may retain modern culture and science in allegiance to Christ.—Possibility of miracles denied by no one.—The same point of view occupied by S. Bernard and M. Renan.—Miracle subject to fair historical inquiry.—The Church bound to be truthful.—All acknowledge this.—No want of liberty exists.—Miracle no violation of "law."—*Miraculous* and *capricious* action not identical.—Admit a God, and you admit "volition" in nature.—New laws are often discovered by science, and not ascribed to caprice.—Unreason has no place in Christian idea of God.—A fixed purpose, undoubtedly, in all signs and wonders.—Miracles acted as scaffolding in building up Monotheism.—When building complete, scaffolding no longer necessary.—St. Paul's life spent in trying to emancipate Gentile world from school-methods of Israel.—The New Testament miracles engendered firm belief in Christ, and conception of Him as image of God's thought concerning man.—Acknowledged beauty of Christ's character.—Christ's spirit has seized us.—Last benediction of the Gospel, "Blessed are they that have not seen, and yet have believed."—Anxious quest about miracles not required of Christians now.—Miracle should come last, not first.—Begin with human nature of Christ, and advance upwards.—"He that is able to receive it let him receive it."—The clergy should look forward, not backward . . . . *Pages* 68—94.

LECTURE V.

THE FALL OF MAN.

Feeling of "shame," a characteristic of the human species.—Pharaoh speaks from the obelisk of seeking peace to his conscience.—No other creatures know what "shame" is.—Impossible to say when sin began.—Yet it must have had a beginning.—On modern as well as ancient theories of descent of man, there was a time when shame had not dawned on him.—There must have been some great transition.—Man hovered for a time "on the razor edge."—Then a fall came.—Christianity and science not divergent.—The fall of man does not contradict hypothesis of evolution.—Denial of moral evil irrational.—Many moral evils exist in human nature which are not bestial.—Problems to be worked out.—Melancholy scientific prognostications of human extinction.—The Church's picture animating and rational.—There shame and fall point to recovery.—Touching poetry of Genesis.—Story suitable for all ages and races of mankind.—Poor success of Milton.—The Fall narrated in prose.—Who could undertake to better this ancient Semitic parable of the origin of sin? *Pages* 95—114.

LECTURE VI.

REDEMPTION.

The Fall and Redemption closely related.—Redemption a metaphorical word.—Metaphor a kind of poetry.—It appeals to the imagination.—Scientific men object that redemption is too much dramatised and thrown into imaginative forms.—But metaphorical language is indispensable.—All representations are confessedly weak and inadequate, but the fact, the reality, remains.—Evil is not totally irreversible.—Assurance of possible recovery is almost too good news to be true.—But the reverse of that assurance were too bad news to be true.—It seems part of our nature at its best to revolt against degrading reign of moral chaos.—To be assured of final shipwreck of humanity would destroy all interest in nature and her ways.

—Some possibility of human redemption must exist.—Religion the most powerful factor for producing moral changes.
—It tamed the barbarous hordes that broke into Roman Empire.—Christianity now binds people together, and redeems them from scourge of perpetual war.—Testimony of Henry George that the salvation of society is in Gospel of Christ.—Human nature to be studied in the nursery.—First mental power awakened is the imagination.—This faculty the easiest to work on.—The good news of Redemption must be told in language to suit the imagination.—Approach there and attention will be arrested.—A new ideal must be supplied.—Lovely ideal set forth in the Gospels.—Handed on by Church.—Her ritual and rhetorical presentation of the subject.—No conflict here with science.—Law of variation works by unexpected appearance of some new type.—Genius sometimes abruptly changes the whole course of world . . . . *Pages* 115—134.

LECTURE VII.

IMMORTALITY.

A subject personally interesting to all.—Recent study of Oriental ways of viewing the world.—But why go backwards in researches after truth?—Eastern ideas of future life.—Limitation of our faculties.—Christianity refuses to reduce this mysterious question into definite terms of the human understanding.—It leaves us free to speculate on all open questions.—Scientific facts not always understood, yet freely taught.—Sympathy therefore asked for the Church which teaches truths not wholly understood.—Explicit faith demanded from no one.—Death alone can reveal the truth.—Eternal or "spiritual" life claims to belong to some higher state of things than we are now familiar with.—Whenever a new class of beings appears new surroundings prepared for them.—Then a new idea buds forth from some parent stock.—A leading specimen appears.—So the second Adam, type and fountain-head of a new race.—They are attached to him, are moulded on His type and became part of His ever-extending Body, the Church.—Nature' transmutations of force.—Fact of Christ's Resurrection.—Difficult to account for success of Christianity without His Resurrection.—Not likely that St. Paul and others were victims of illusion.—This aids us to picture the future life.—Can we believe that all men, good and bad, pass into annihilation?—Beautiful poetry of the Apocalypse.—Temptation to forget that it is poetry and to put a construction on its language which it is not meant to convey.—Unbroken chain of life in the past.—Vain curiosity about the future.—Why not leave all in God's hands?—Amazing wealth of forms displayed by Him in Nature.—St. Paul's teaching agrees with science. — Our present life full of mystery ; and ourselves a standing parable of life victorious over death . . . . *Pages* 135—164.

LECTURE VIII.

CONCLUSION.

All have passed through much perplexity.—But even "little faith" is not without reward.—It has life and will grow.—The present a transition period.—Doubt appointed to some persons as their schooling.—Patience needed.—Science has engendered no form of religious worship of its own.—Positivism idealises man instead of the Cosmos.—Addressed to the more refined classes.—Secularism to the lower classes.—The West too prosaic for great religious enthusiasms.—Loyalty to the Power that rules the world bids us accept the Christian system. — Our organised Christianity has carried us through twelve centuries of as sacred a history as ever belonged to any people.—There is no contradiction between Science and Christianity.—Free inquiry is a watch-word of the Gospel.—Yet some "system" is required to save the soul from shipwreck and ruin.—Christian teachers look for sympathy and patience from men of science.—Only the moral qualities of Faith, Hope, and Charity required—things capable of infinite gradations.
Pages 165—181.

THE SCIENTIFIC OBSTACLES

TO

CHRISTIAN BELIEF.

LECTURE I.

HISTORICAL INTRODUCTION.

1 Cor. i. 22 : "The Jews require a sign, and the Greeks seek after wisdom."

Rom. iii. 29 : "Is He the God of the Jews only? Is He not also of the Gentiles?"

THERE can be no question, I think, that the foundations of Christian belief have been, during the latter half of the nineteenth century, very rudely shaken and disturbed. No one who either reads or thinks, or who observes carefully what is going on around him, can well avoid this conclusion. For not only in private intercourse with each other do men of culture and education acknowledge their difficulties, but so much is unbelief in the air that even vulgar irreligion has felt encouraged to be jubilant and noisy.[1]

---

[1] The most remarkable and exaggerated specimen of "jubilant" irreligion comes to us, with many other exaggerations, from the other side of the Atlantic. In Colonel Ingersoll—who ought to be a hearty, manly Christian, of the type of

LECT. I.

Public caricatures of sacred things have been attempted: and one may hear in many a debating society blasphemies openly vented,

Bishop Hacket with his maxim, "Serve God and be cheerful" —we have (at present) a powerful speaker against Christianity. His "orations" are fresh and delightful; they are couched in high-flown, poetical prose; they sound like Emerson adapted to a popular platform. But the Christianity he opposes is a fossil thing. If it survive anywhere, it must be in some remote conventicles in the backwoods of America. His most impassioned appeals simply demand a right to think and speak freely, which every sentence shows that he already possesses. Is there not something a trifle unreal, and therefore ludicrous, in such posturing as this: "I do not pretend to have fathomed the abyss, nor to have floated on outstretched wings level with the dim heights of thought. 1 simply plead for freedom: I ask for light and air for the souls of men. I say, Take off those chains; break those manacles; free those limbs; release that brain! I plead for the right to think, to reason, to investigate."—(*Religion of the Future*, 14th edition, p. 17.) "Priests tell us there is a god somewhere in heaven, who objects to a human being thinking and expressing his thoughts."—(*How Man makes Gods*, p. 163.) The Christian's answer is: "All this is ancient history, and not always quite accurate history: for instance, 'The Epistles are addressed to nobody. ... The Testament, as it now is, was not written for hundreds of years after the apostles were dust.'"—(*What must we do to be Saved?* p. 198.) It is pitiful to see such power and energy wasted against a "man of straw," especially when the orator is virtually a Christian, if he only knew it. "The meanest hut," he says, "with love in it is a palace fit for the gods. ... You cannot be so poor that you cannot help somebody. ... It is not necessary to be rich: joy is wealth. ... There is neither in my heart nor on my lips a sneer for the hopeful, loving souls who believe that over all there is a Being who, in some way, will reclaim and glorify every one of the children of men. ...

which can only proceed upon the confident presumption that, in the eternal conflict between Reason and Faith, Faith is at present undergoing a series of defeats, and that Christianity is entangled with such legacies of un-reason from the past that the intractable knot admits of no easy solution, but must be violently cut. Another extremely suggestive phenomenon also points the same way. It appears that great numbers of *women* nowadays are affected by unbelief: and many a life is made restless and unhappy by the dissatisfaction which arises when such natural and congenial duties as those of teaching young children, visiting the poor, attendance at church, are thwarted by some interior cross-current of thought, whispering doubt and self-suspicion of hypocrisy.[1] It is high time, therefore, that

For the man Christ I have infinite respect: the place where man has died for man is holy ground : to that great and serene man I gladly pay the tribute of my admiration and my tears." To one who can say all this, Jesus Himself would have replied, "Thou art not far from the Kingdom of God."

[1] I speak here from personal knowledge. But the experience of hundreds will justify what I say. There is, in these days, an ever-increasing number of highly educated women who deeply lament the difficulties of Christian belief, and who are as far as possible from feeling, with Mrs. Besant, "No religion has ever brought so glad a message to the world as this good news of Atheism." Read the *Life of Miss Martineau*, the *Life of Miss Carpenter*, the *Life of Ellen Watson*, "*We Two*" (a novel), and the *Life of Annie Keary*, who touchingly asks,

LECT. I.

Christendom aroused itself to grapple boldly with an unsolved problem which is working such mischievous results; and that the question were honestly asked, and fairly answered, *What are the main obstacles which debar our own generation from the happiness of tranquil Christian belief?*

Now the first step in this inquiry should be the historical one—How is it that the present failure of belief has come to pass? For if it should appear that the present distress has arisen from no fault of our own, but simply by the lapse of time, and in consequence of the ordinary laws of intellectual progression, the discovery will aid in restoring serenity to troubled minds.[1] It will

---

"May it not be that the souls which are meant to flower most gloriously towards God have to grope about a long time in doubt and uncertainty?"—(p. 206.) If the Christian clergy have become too feeble or too timid to minister to minds like these, degeneracy must indeed have set in. "Degeneres animos timor arguit," says Virgil: while a real "faith makes all men brave," says Origen (Cels. i. 11). "I have shrunk from going to clergymen" (said Altiora); "they appear to adapt their religion to the social requirements by which they are surrounded, instead of going in for the highest thing, *coûte que coûte.*"—(Oliphant's *Altiora Peto*, i. 190.) But "Ein wahrer Priester strebt den schlafenden Keim der besseren Menschheit zu wecken, die Liebe zum höheren zu entzünden, das gemeine Leben in ein edleres zu verwandeln."—(Schleiermacher, *Rede über Religion*, p. 150.)

[1] This hopeful feeling seems to have taken possession of many thoughtful minds. "These times of renewing and regeneration

show how, by causes we could not control, our planet has (so to speak) been swept on into new environments; so that, naturally and inevitably, the old bearings have somewhat changed their places, and the old "evidences" have in many cases lost something of their evidential value. It will also show how each successive generation has its own difficulties to encounter. It will recall to remembrance the fact that, if perplexities about belief form the special trial of our own

LECT. I.

of human nature seem to occur at intervals, according to some law which Science has not yet fathomed. . . . And upon such a period of renovation there are signs that we may now be entering."—(Graham, *Creed of Science*, 1881, p. 281.) "There never was a time when the fundamental doctrines of Christianity could be more boldly proclaimed, or when they could better secure the respect and arrest the interest of Science."—(Drummond, *Natural Law in the Spiritual World*, 7th edition, 1884, p. 162.) For this benefit some thanks are due to the much-despised previous century, from which "the nineteenth century has received a rich bequest, though never was an heir more ungrateful to his benefactor."—(Strauss, *Essays*, French trans., p. 60.) Indeed in every man his "last thoughts are but the result of changes dating far back in his own individual history, or having their roots in the modes of mental or vital activity of his ancestors."—(Laycock, *Mind and Brain*, 2nd edition, 1869, i. 2.) For—to quote the oldest and most piquant of modern books on this subject—"A man's past selves are living in him at this moment, with the accumulated life of centuries. 'Do this, this, this, which we have done and found our profit in it,' cry the souls of his forefathers within him. Faint are the far ones, coming and going as the sound of bells: loud and clear are the near ones. . . . Our *own* experience indeed !"—(Samuel Butler, *Life and Habit*, 1878, p. 52.)

day, still it is not the first time that Knowledge and Faith have been found difficult of adjustment, nor the first time that people's moral courage and religious loyalty have been tested by doubt. Nay, more than that: it will reveal how certain generations seem privileged to settle questions that have been accumulating, perhaps, for a thousand years. For just as, watching the play of waves along the shore, we often notice that some rhythmic law of weight and impetus not only propels wave after wave in sheets of fretted foam at our feet, but also gathers in each seventh billow (as it is said) all surplus energy and momentum, so we may detect a rhythm in the history of thought. Whence it happens that on the skill and courage and readiness of certain people at certain times may hang suspended the destinies of the whole future and of all mankind. Life is difficult at such epochs. Yet who would not prefer to live at such turning-points in the world's history, and to form part of such an elect generation as that? What would we not, every one of us, give to have had a share in defending Europe from Asiatic supremacy at Marathon, or in crushing Varus and his imperial legions on the free soil of our Fatherland, or in shattering the Spanish Armada under Queen Elizabeth! Well, in the conflicts of thought, too, similar honours are to be gained, and similar benefits to mankind are to be achieved. In both cases the same qualities are essential to success, viz., confidence in our cause, and self-sacrificing bravery in maintaining it. May we Englishmen of the nineteenth century show as much patience, skill, industry, and courage in this field of mental strife as our countrymen have always hitherto displayed whenever " Duty, stern daughter of the voice of God," has summoned them to personal energy and mutual trust![1]

(1.) Now on looking back over the annals of the Christian Church, the larger waves of (what may

[1] This new form of "struggle" which has devolved upon us at the present day strikes all observers. The struggle for survival "now rages as violently and inexorably on the domain of morals as it formerly did on the physical field."—(Büchner, *Man in the Past*, &c., English trans., 1872, p. 158.) "The Christian faith, in the judgment both of its enemies and of its friends, is at this moment threatened by dangers as formidable as any which it has ever had to confront during the whole course of its history."—(Dale, *On the Atonement*, 7th edition, 1878, p. 27.) But Continental Romanism can never grapple with such dangers as these; when "La Science cherche le mot de l'univers, que l'Église Catholique a laissé s'obscurcir."—(E. Burnouf, *Science des Religions*, 3rd edition, 1876, p. 432.) It is English Christendom which is called upon to meet this new foe, worthy of its steel. But then it must be fearless. It should take to heart a late warning: "Something has arrested development. What? The retrospectiveness, the fear of ceasing to be what it originally was, which seizes an institution when it has begun to be uncertain why it exists."—(*Natural Religion*, 1882, p. 223.)

be called) her "scientific" controversy seem to have gathered themselves up mainly at four epochs. The first arose so early as the end of the first century, and it taxed severely the skill and courage even of the Apostolic age. It was the great wave of Gnosticism; of which perhaps MARCION, in the second century, is the ablest and most prominent representative. Christ had now come and gone. A quantity of new and surprising facts had, by His appearance, been abruptly added to the world's stock of experiences. And Judaism was content naïvely to employ them—as we see so vividly in the writings of St. James, and in most of the early Christian literature—in fugitive, homiletic, and epistolary forms. But no sooner did Christianity come in contact with the acute and logical Greek mind, than it found itself at once in collision with a whole outside world of European philosophies and sciences; and these could not fail to exercise a profound influence upon the method employed by its preachers. Track, for instance, St. Paul's progress westward; observe the singular transitions of thought which he is undergoing at every step; contrast the thoroughly Jewish cast of his Epistles to the *Thessalonians* with the Greek tone and the philosophic colour of his later Epistles to the *Romans, Ephesians* and *Colossians;* and then bring the last surviving Apostle, St. John, into the field, and notice his "logos doctrine" and his other philosophical speculations;—and we cannot fail to become aware that we see already the first stirrings of the great intellectual Gnostic movement even upon the pages of the New Testament itself. And if we carry our studies a little further on, and open the history of the second century, we discover the movement in its full onward swing.

Gnosticism was, in fact, a wave of speculation much like that which stirs us at the present day. Christianity had already been morally and spiritually accepted by the great mass of those to whom it was preached; and now it was in process of intellectually establishing itself. It was feeling earnestly around for a suitable body, or logical system of thought, in which to inshrine its spirit, its new emotions, its vague ideas, engendered once for all by the abrupt appearance of Christ upon the world's stage. One thing only could spoil the process: and that was the prevalence of impatience and of self-conceit. And when, at length, they did prevail, then the whole movement went astray and lost itself in wild and futile attempts to clothe Christianity in the motley garments of second-century science. Pairs of Æons, male and female, were invented: a vast system of emanation was thought out: the personal GOD became an abstraction, an "abyss," a "silence": the world was condemned as a huge blunder, the work of a secondary creative power removed by many long stages from God: and its recovery to reason and good order was set in motion by the direct descent of another Æon, Christ, from heaven commissioned by the Supreme Being to counteract and reverse the mistakes of the Demiurge, the inferior god of the Old Testament dispensation. Such wild work as this was rightly characterised by St. Paul as a "science falsely so called." Its ideas were crude and whimsical; while yet it presumed to give itself the airs of a universal and permanent presentment of truth. And so, clothing itself in a Christian dress, Gnosticism ventured forth to proclaim itself to the world as the unadulterated religion of pure reason.

Confronted for the first time with these strange intellectual pretensions, it is highly interesting and instructive to observe how the Church comported herself. And it is satisfactory to find that, guided by the spirit of truthfulness and of tolerance, she first gladly embraced and imbedded in her system all that was good in Gnosticism; and then, having done so, was bold to warn and rebuke those who pushed their speculations into extravagance, to announce that the Church declined to follow them, and to foretell that Gnosticism, thus taught, was in the fair way to become a "heresy." Clement of Alexandria, early in the third century, tried his best to re-Christianise Gnosticism, and to secure to the Church the great advantage of an alliance, instead of a warfare, with the science (such as it was) of the day. But his efforts were in vain. The hard intellectual spirit refused the easy yoke of Christ; and, withdrawing itself erelong in Neo-platonism and Manichæanism, depleted the Church of much intellectual power and prepared for Christendom the long death of "the dark Ages."

(2.) Pass over a thousand years: and now another wave of controversy with Science has accumulated and must be dealt with. Eleven centuries have come and gone since Christ appeared in the world. And during that vast lapse of time the ancient civilisation, with all its treasures of culture and thought, had died and been buried. The hordes of barbarism had broken in upon its entrenched and imposing order, and the classic world had gone down in hideous ruin and confusion. But by the end of the eleventh century a new order had sprung up and become established. The feudal and monastic systems began to restore peace and settled government; leisure returned and thought

LECT. revived.[1] And then, at the fortunate moment, the
L. stores of Eastern learning and of Arabian science
were poured out at the feet of the Western
nations; and in ABELARD, and many others, a
wave of doubtful omen began to raise its threatening head, scornful once more of the Church's
traditional ways, and threatening another attempt
to reconstruct theology upon independent lines,
and to elevate the mere fleeting science of a day
into a religion for all days. And what was the
Church's behaviour now? It was the same as
before. She addressed herself to "refuse the evil

[1] It is curious to observe how, in unexpected quarters, a tardy justice is being done to the Church, as, in fact, the prudent nurse and not the enraged enemy of Science. "In Religion let us recognise the high merit that, from the beginning, it has dimly discerned the ultimate verity, and has never ceased to insist upon it. . . . Each higher religious creed, rejecting those definite and simple interpretations of Nature previously given, has become more religious by doing this."— (H. Spencer, *First Principles*, 4th edition, 1880, p. 99.) "Whatever Science may have done to confirm man's idea of the unity of Nature, Theology had more to do with it."—(Duke of Argyll, *Unity of Nature*, 1884, p. 2.) "There has been a tendency among modern thinkers to dwell upon the greed, the craft, the obscurantism of (so-called) spiritual rule, and to represent the priesthood as the hereditary enemy of progress. It may be asserted, with at least equal truth, that priests have been its chief promoters."—(*Westminster Review*, October, 1883, p. 422.) And even in Polynesia the fact has been acknowledged. "Ordinairement c'était ces collèges de prêtres qui conservaient les connaissances nautiques et astronomiques vraiment remarquables."—(Reville, *Religions des Peuples non civilisés*, 1883, ii. 77.)

and choose the good." And while enthusiastically accepting the new aids of heathen *logic* and *metaphysics* which Providence had suddenly placed at her disposal, she declined to embrace or to be responsible for other parts of the Aristotelian philosophy, and especially for his unmanageable *physical* science.[1] No ; she would wait (if

LECT.
I.

---

[1] It is well known how deeply the school divines were indebted to Aristotle's logic and metaphysics for their fine-spun Theology. The notion of Transubstantiation, for instance, is wholly derived from that heathen source ; though it may have received an odd sanction from certain epicuræan speculations. For instance : " Hominis esse specie Deos, confitendum est ; nec tamen ea species ' corpus ' est, sed quasi-corpus,—nec habet ' sanguinem,' sed quasi-sanguinem."—(Cicero, *De Nat. Deorum*, lib. i. § 18.) But both Innocent III. in the thirteenth century, and Urban V. in the fourteenth, firmly refused leave to the University of Paris to study Aristotle's physical writings. (Bp. Hampden, *Bampton Lectures*, p. 444.) In sober truth, surely the world was not then ripe for any worthy physical science ; and Dr. Büchner should have withheld his commonplace sneer, that "the Christian Middle Age was the sworn enemy of all study of nature."—(*Animal Physiology*, French trans., p. 5.) Grostête, the noble Bishop of Lincoln († 1253), especially encouraged the establishment of the Franciscans at Oxford, because of their free cultivation of natural science. His pupil, the celebrated Roger Bacon († 1293), pursued with ardour—though with a wild extravagance which caused him to be charged with " magic "—the study of Nature, the knowledge of whose laws he declared to be " the true magic."—(Laugen, ap. *Histor. Zeitschrift*, 1884, p. 442.) In 1312, Pope Clement V.—following Bacon's lead—ordered Hebrew and Arabic (the physician's languages) to be studied in the European universities. And in 1582, Pope Gregory XIII. reformed the Calendar, as Roger Bacon had advised three hundred years before. At

necessary) for another thousand years. What was lapse of time to her! And can we, looking back from our present scientific vantage-ground, say that such patience was either ill-advised or wrong?

(3.) Pass over another five hundred years, and yet a third tremendous accumulation of threatening Science has to be dealt with. By the end of the sixteenth century the reformation of the Church had been fully accomplished: the New World had been discovered and partly settled: the ancient classical civilisation had once more come forth into vivid light: and every mind that could think, every heart that could feel, throughout all Christendom, was vibrating with pardonable pride at the new powers which mankind had suddenly displayed and the new wonders which God had almost miraculously revealed.[1] The time, in short,

length, in 1620, Francis Bacon published the ripe fruit of a thirty years' study in his *Novum Organum*, or new method of dealing with Nature; viz., by "renouncing *notions* and beginning to form an acquaintance with *things*."—(*Nov. Org.*, ed. Pickering, p. 16.) Thus the patience which checked crude efforts till "the fulness of time was come," at last received its reward.

[1] The joy, the καύχησις, with which the "Humanists" of the sixteenth century welcomed their emancipation from Scholastic Theology, may be compared with the similar "exultation" of St. Paul and of his school at their emancipation from the Jewish Law; and with the heartfelt thankfulness which irradiates every modern student of Nature at his emancipation from the dreary formulas of Puritan Divinity.

had come round again for the appearance of the old danger and the old opportunity—the "danger" For the intellectual aspect of this "joy" see Bacon's *Novum Organum*, Part I—with his remarkable reference to the recent opening-up of "our new Continent." For its æsthetic aspect, study the Renaissance pictures in the National Gallery. For its comic aspect, skim through Von Hutten's *Epistolæ Obscurorum Virorum* and Erasmus' ironical *Praise of Folly*. At the present day the feelings of non-Christian students seem a little mixed. In Mr. Matthew Arnold they are merely sad :—

"The sea of Faith
Was once too at the full ; and round Earth's shore
Lay, like the folds of a bright girdle, furled :
But now I only hear
Its melancholy, long withdrawing roar."

Prof. Clifford, with all his spring and brightness, owns to a deeper regret :—"The loss of belief is a very painful loss. We have felt, with utter loneliness, that the Great Companion is dead."—(*Essays*, ii. 247.) Mr. Stuart-Glennie sinks deeper: " Very far are we from being the first who have experienced the agony of discovered delusion."—(*In the Morning-land*, i. 378.) While the Duke of Somerset confesses to being "excruciated with doubt."—(*Modern Scepticism*, p.144.) Others again are jubilant. Dr. Büchner cries—and he is followed by Mrs. Besant—"Atheism alone leads to freedom, to reason, to progress."—(*Der Gottesbegriff*, p. 45.) Some are scornful :—

" But in the reign of Science you are born.
Theology, with pomp and riches, yet
Sits mumbling, droning, in his padded chair,
Gouty, asthmatic, ailing every way.
A young audacious voice rings through the land."
(*Evil May-day*, Macmillan's Magazine, November, 1878.)

and some even are comical :—" Gavroche arrivant d'emblée et avec si peu de peine au dernier mot de la philosophie—c'est bien dur à penser !"—(Renan, *Souvenirs*, 9th edition, p. 155.) Amid all these curiosities of un-Christian emotion, the Christian Student of Nature remains simply calm, thankful, and hopeful.

of crude and wild and self-confident attempts to reconstruct Theology from its basis and to elevate the mere ideas of the sixteenth contury into a Religion for all time; and the "opportunity" for weaving into the web of Christian teaching some of the new bright threads that the progress of discovery had placed at the Church's disposal. Around the name of FRANCIS BACON all our memories of this most deeply important time instinctively gather. In his works, and especially in the first part of his *Novum Organum*, all the stirring thought of the time is mirrored and the best science of the Elizabethan golden-age arrays itself in shapes of brilliant promise for the future.[1]

But ere long the shadows deepen also. Deism and various other forms of unbelief display themselves; and the old error is yet a third time repeated, in rash attempts to reconstruct a Religion out of the over-estimated data of a transient phase of thought. "Patience!" was again the warning voice of Christian good sense; "the sublime and the ridiculous, the rational and the irrational, the splendidly, fruitfully true and the absurdly, desperately false, are never far removed from each other. It were a grievous pity unawares to cross the line that separates them, and by too

[1] See Dean Church's brief and admirable *Life of Francis Bacon* (1884) and criticism of his work.

much haste and over-confidence now to spoil the future of the world." But, in spite of all such warnings, the future was (to a great extent) compromised. Christendom was thoughtlessly riven into a hundred divisions; and seeds of unbelief were sown, which should ruinously fructify in a coming "age of reason," and produce at length the nameless horrors and absurdities of the French Revolution.[1]

(4.) And now, in our own time, yet another crisis has gathered, and a similar wave-crest of threatening mischief to Christian belief towers menacingly above all the smaller controversies of the day. For, once more, a great revelation of new truths has been granted to the world; and, in the renowned name of DARWIN, Science

---

[1] "En France on attaqua avec une sorte de fureur la religion chrétienne sans essayer même de mettre une autre religion à sa place." (De Tocqueville, *L'ancien Régime et la Révolution:* 3rd edition, p. 251.) Contrast the moderate, regretful, and "almost Christian" tone which, amid the freer air of the nineteenth century, characterises even French unbelief. "Il est de toute nécessité que chacun garde sa foi dans son cœur; et permette à son intelligence de suivre les voies que la raison lui ouvre."— (E. Burnouf, *Science des Religions,* 3rd edition, p. 4.) "Je regrettais par moments de n'être pas Protestant, afin de pouvoir être philosophe sans cesser d'être chrétien. Je cherchais à croire ; mais je ne pouvais. Oh oui, mon ami, ces jours compteront dans ma vie ; s'ils n'en furent les plus décisifs, ils en furent au moins les plus pénibles."—(Renan, *Souvenirs,* 9th edition, pp. 292, 394.)

honours the laborious achievements of a hundred patient observers, and suspects the advent of perhaps a new Religion for mankind. The word "religion" may seem a strong one: but it is, I think, justified by the unmeasured language used nowadays by some of Mr. Darwin's most devoted followers—the disciples, as usual, far outstripping the master. For instance, Dr. Büchner (the celebrated spokesman of this school in Germany) thus buoyantly unfurls the banner of his crude materialism, and proclaims the approaching conversion of a transient phase of physical science into a Religion : " The sciencemen (he says) of the last generation committed the grave fault of abstaining from generalisation, and contented themselves with the ceaseless accumulation of facts. Nowadays—thanks to the appearance of the Evolution theory—a *philosophical* [he means a theological] movement has been imported into the domain of the natural sciences." [1] And if we ask what religious form

---

[1] Thus even Strauss "answers the question, 'Are we still Christians?' quite unreservedly, No; the question, however, 'Have we still a religion?' with a conditional Yes. It depends, that is to say, whether our feeling of dependence as regards the universe and its laws is to be accounted a 'religion' or not. A cult we shall no longer build upon this feeling; but it still has a moral effect and is connected with a certain piety."—Lange, *History of Materialism*, English trans., 1881, iii. 329.) But some Naturalists, it appears, go further; and Dr. Löwenthal, at

this new philosophy of Materialism is to take, the answer is given a few pages further back:— "The Sun is the supreme source of all our activity, both physical and intellectual: and this truth of itself suffices to reduce to nothing all the Theological interpretations of the Universe. Yes: were a Religion of Nature still possible, we could not choose an object more worthy of our worship than the luminary adored by our ancestors."[1] In short, we are invited to return to Baal worship once more! But surely that magnificent sweep

Leipsic, in 1865 tried to establish a "cogitant" community, with a downright worship of Thought and Knowledge. Dr. Reich, at Neuwied, in 1873, started a sort of "Church of Humanity," with processions, hymns, drums, trumpets, organs, and carillons, under an organised priesthood. (*Ibid*, p. 295.) Comte, as we all know, vainly attempted the same kind of absurdity.

[1] Büchner, *Light and Life*, French trans., 1883, p. 6.—Contrast the sober, yet elevated and poetical tone of Professor Tyndall, years before, in his celebrated *Lectures on Heat.*—(1863, p. 431.) "All terrestrial power is drawn from the Sun. . . . The Sun comes to us as 'heat,' he quits us as 'heat'; and between his entrance and departure the multiform powers of our globe appear. They are all special forms of solar power. Presented rightly to the mind, the discoveries and generalisations of modern science constitute a 'poem,' more sublime than has ever yet been addressed to the intellect and imagination of man." Yes,—on account of the enormous and astonishing complexity of its harmonies. But, viewed in relation to the time and the surroundings whence it came, perhaps the primæval "Psalm of the Divine Creation," in the Book of Genesis, is far more wonderful and (in its simplicity) equally sublime.

LECT.
I.

of Christian thought, which passes at one bound beyond, not merely the sun, but the very outermost star that feebly glimmers in our telescopes, and which disdains the biggest material galaxy of hydrogen, sodium, and iron that ever flickered in the sky as so much "dust of the balance" when compared with the sublime idea of GOD needs not to lower its triumphant ensign to a religion of dead things, nor to dwarf its stately worship of the Omnipotent and the Eternal into a cultus of the reigning notion of the hour about vibratory movements called "heat." This were indeed to surrender the grandest, the most expansive, and the most supremely rational[1] conception of the Universe that has ever yet been presented to mankind, in favour of a mere pedantry of the laboratory, a religion with as little inspiration in it as that of the Rabbis or the Schoolmen.

[1] All science is, and ought to be, impersonal : all religion is, and must be, personal. It is impossible therefore for Science, by itself, to generate any rational form of Religion ; while Religion—superadding (as it does) to the conceptions of Science the notion of Conscious Will in the Universe—redeems these conceptions from the charge of representing the Universe as a dead, mechanical, infra-human thing, and at once makes it human, rational, instinct with consciousness and life. Now this grand thought—embodying the Pantheism of Spinoza and something more—is expressed by Christianity in its doctrine of the Creation and sustentation of all things by the Divine Word or Reason, "by whom all things were made."

And now one question remains—and it is of the deepest importance to both Science and Religion that it should be thought out to a reasonable issue. It is this: *By what law of the human mind is it that these successive epochs of doubt occur?* What is the cause, not of the mere daily plash and angry break of trivial controversies, but of the rise and menacing accumulation of these larger and more intermittent conflicts? Are they to be explained as tidal waves of mental oscillation, bearing on their mighty rise and fall the whole tumult of our local storms, and swayed by some external force that is not terrestrial merely, but of a larger and supernatural order? Or do they obey some natural law of the human mind? *Their law, I believe, is to be sought for in the natural play and counteraction of two polar forces in the brain.* For we possess, on the one hand, an analysing, subdividing, restless questioning-power in the INTELLECT; we have, on the other hand, a formative, simplifying, synthetic power in the IMAGINATION. The movements of the *intellect* are rapid, incessant, mordant, disintegrating, and, by themselves, merely destructive. They are like the unwearied agencies which decompose organic bodies or wear down mountain-chains. Interminable and illimitable investigation is their

LECT.
I.

proper function; and without their salutary check forms of thought once established would remain eternally fixed; customs and dogmas and formulæ once accepted would refuse all change and all purification; and to every offered reform an indolent Conservatism would oppose a bar of finality, and in imperious tones would reply "*non possumus*,"—we will not and we can not (except by accumulation of fresh dogmas and formulæ) submit to any change.

Yet, on the other hand, when allowed to act by themselves without restraint from the *imagination*, the forces of the intellect are irrational and destructive. Let any one study the curious phenomenon of Buddhism—that revolt against the unbridled imaginativeness of Brahmanism by preaching salvation through pure intellectual analysis—and then he will understand what injury may be done by a one-sided use of the human faculties.[1] For if truth is to be reached, *all* the human mind, and not merely *half* of it, must be employed. Action and reaction, analysis and synthesis, diastole and systole, are essential to the healthy working of

[1] The most easily accessible works on Buddhism are the two slight, but interesting, manuals by Rhys Davids (S.P.C.K.) and by Bishop Titcomb (Religious Tract Society). For further study, consult Hardy's *Eastern Monachism*, Köppen's *Buddha*, St. Hilaire's *Buddhisme*, Max Müller's *Sacred Books of the East*, &c.

the mind, just as they are to the well-being of the body.

And so we have reached, at last, the common ground on which both science and religion may stand together; we have gained the initial point from which all successful work in either department must needs take its start. That common ground, that initial point, is FAITH,—faith in the sufficiency of the human mind, and faith in the true and kindly leading of that exterior Cosmic power, which now stimulates our intellect by the revelation of new discoveries, and now calls on our imagination to bestir itself and to re-form its old conceptions in the light of these new discoveries. It is only by honestly acting in this "faith" that we can each of us "serve our own generation by the will of God," and can carry into effect our Lord's injunctions to "bring forth, out of the treasures committed to our stewardship, things both new and old." It is by this "faith" that mountains of seeming difficulty are easily removed; and that, even amid the desert of surrounding scepticism, a highway is prepared for further advances towards the attainment of truth. For every argument must begin with some axiom; and, as the prophet said of old, "if ye will not *believe*, ye shall not be established."[1]

---

[1] Isaiah vii. 9.

LECTURE II.

GOD.

Colossians i. 15: "The image of the invisible God."

IF the principles laid down in the previous lecture are correct, and it can be substantiated that all rational thinking is invariably the result of two mental factors working harmoniously together, the INTELLECT and the IMAGINATION—it becomes easy to understand how opposite deflections from reason and good sense may arise on any subject whatever; and, among the rest, on Religion. For, as heathen and Christian thinkers agree in affirming, truth usually lies midway between extreme statements. And so, while one class of errors—pointing towards superstition—will be caused by excessive reliance on the imagination alone, another class of errors—pointing towards atheism—will be as certainly generated by too exclusive a reliance on the bare intellect. In both cases, balance and counterpoise are wanting, and one-sidedness is the result. And, inasmuch as the over-imaginative mind is naturally prone to feed itself on thoughts and scenes which afford it nourishment, and so, unawares, to aggravate its own malady; and the hard intellectual character, scorning the apparent untruthfulness of legend, poetry, and art, is tempted to immerse itself ever deeper in mere criticism and analysis; it follows that the angle of divergence between these two classes of minds may easily go on widening until reconciliation becomes impossible. And then, perhaps, war is at last declared. Hard words and uncharitable insinuations embitter the conflict. And the result may be, ere long, that violent contrast which shocks the traveller in so many foreign cities, where emblems of gross and puerile fanaticism are flaunted on one side of the street, while a hostile array of atheistic literature and blasphemous caricature is paraded on the other.[1]

---

[1] The streets of Brussels were mainly in the writer's thoughts. And there, since these words were written, a most violent conflict has broken out between the "clerical" and the "liberal" party. Indeed no country is free from these convulsions which has allowed its Christianity to become (as Coleridge would say) Petrified. Perpetual self-adaptation to surroundings is the universal law of life, as Mr. Spencer has well pointed out; and that which refuses to conform to this law is a failure, and is on

LECT. II.

Happy those nations and churches that are wise enough to soften the asperities of such a conflict; to reform with bold fidelity whatever from time to time may on either side need reforming; and, by courtesy and mutual tolerance, to maintain on foot, that surest guarantee of peace and national stability, a large central body of fairly unanimous opinion, midway between smaller extreme parties of irreconcilable violence and of extravagant dogmatism.

But this inestimable blessing can only be secured at one price. There must be sincere and repeated efforts at a mutual understanding. And, therefore, while "physicians"[1] are bound, for

its way to extinction. Dean Stanley gives a curious account of the Russian "Starovers," or Dissenters from the Greek Church, who take their stand on absolute immobility.—(*Eastern Church*, p. 471.) And in England the "seventh-day Baptists," and other religious societies, present the same melancholy spectacle. But even St. Paul became "all things to all men, that he might save some."

[1] It were very convenient if this word could be restored to its original meaning, and could take the place of "scientist," "philosopher," "naturalist," "professor of physical science," and other cumbrous or ambiguous phrases; and could henceforth express simply "a student of Nature." A beginning has already been made, for instance, by Büchner (*Light and Life*, French trans., p. 202) and by others. It is obvious that Law, Physic, and Divinity still fairly represent—though viewed on their practical and useful side—the three great departments of study; viz. the ways of man, of nature, and of God: and that these three words exhaust all the possibilities of human know-

their part, to pursue science without unmannerly
assaults on religion, "theologians" are equally
bound, on their part, to put no irritating obstacles
in the way of science. Their duty is rather to
irradiate with a touching human beauty, and to
explain in terms of human morality, that vast
un-human, inscrutable universe, whose structure
science has laid bare.[1] For the work of religion

ledge. For, with every respect for the subtle and thoughtful writer known as "Dionysius the Areopagite," it is impossible to think that "what the doctors have seen by a divine intuition" concerning the Angelic Hierarchy can be accounted as any certain information about another world.

[1] How any naturalist, with a heart to feel for others' sufferings, can study Nature's ways without craving for some extraneous explanation of her "in-humanity," is a mystery beyond solution. For, as Kant long ago truly remarked, "the study of nature, by itself, leads to no theological results."—(*Critik of Pure Reason*, p. 390.) And thinkers like Schopenhauer and J. S. Mill concur with the ancient gnostics in feeling the evils of the world to be a most terrible enigma for man to contemplate. The latter bluntly declares that "nearly all the things, which men are hanged or imprisoned for doing to one another, are Nature's everyday performances."—(*Essays on Religion*, p. 28.) Take the insect world: Darwin "found on one sundew-leaf the remains of thirteen insects. The number thus annually slaughtered must be prodigious."—(*Insectivorous Plants*, p. 2.) "Viviparous flies produce 22,000 at a birth;" soon, but for wholesale destruction, "we should have 2,000 decillions."—(Van Bryssal, *Population of an Old Pear-tree*, p. 165.) Or take the animal world: "Early in the autumn, swarms of lemmings [a sort of rat, a few inches long] mount the steep slopes of Heimdals-ho, on their way to the coast; where the harrassed crowd—thinned by the unceasing attacks of the wolf, the fox, the dog, and even

is very greatly imaginative work. Its function is to idealise and to personify. But the hard scientific intellect is, by itself, impotent to advance one step beyond "structure." Dissection (so to speak) of the great dead body of the Cosmos is its proper duty and delight. Analysis is its work; and it becomes uneasy in the presence of anything that seems to defy analysis. The very sixty-three elementary substances are regarded but as conquests deferred, virgin-peaks that the climber has set his heart on one day scaling.

the reindeer, pursued by the eagle, hawk, and owl, and never spared by man himself, yet still a vast multitude—plunges into the Atlantic Ocean and perishes."—(*Popular Science Review*, April, 1877.) Add to this the graphic but harrowing account of the seeding of the bamboo, and its results, in Robinson's *My Indian Garden* (p. 193), and study the multifarious engines of death and destruction, the "tooth and claw," to be seen in any Natural History Museum. It is idle to console oneself with Schopenhauer's easy dictum, "Hier wirkt der Wille in seiner Ursprünglichkeit — also erkenntnisslos. Man versteht die Sprache der Natur nicht, weil sie zu einfach ist."—(*Uber den Willen in der Natur*, 4th edition, pp. 55, 58.) It is still idler to regard, with J. S. Mill, "Nature and life as the product of a struggle between contriving Goodness and an intractable material, or a Principle of evil, as was the doctrine of the Manichæans." —(*Essays*, p. 116.) Unless we give up the problem altogether, it is far more rational to "humanise" the inhuman phenomenon by carrying it boldly up into the conscious, but inscrutable Will which, for ends unknown to us, determines all things. (*Rom.* viii. 20.) Such "subjection in hope" is within the experience of every child, every servant, every subject; the other explanations fall outside all human experience and verification.

Nay, even the ultimate atoms of matter themselves are viewed with suspicion as tainted with the heresy of finality, and as making pretensions to an inviolability which it is not in the habit of science to accord to any person or thing whatever. Thus the work of the pure *Intellect* is throughout analytical and discriminative. Like that kindred but vaster cosmic power which is described in Hebrews iv. 12—it is "quick and powerful and sharper than any two-edged sword, piercing even to the dividing asunder of soul and spirit and of the joints and marrow." And whenever, weary of its eternal investigations, it would pause and clothe with shapeliness and beauty its heaps of crude materials, it is obliged at once to awaken its companion and to borrow help from the *Imagination.* It must summon that wondrous artist which can restore unity to the incoherent mass of details, can transmute a sequence of phenomena into a "law," a stream of tendencies into a "purpose," a succession of changes into an "evolution," a series of events into a "history;" and, in short, can make dead things live.

But how can the imagination make dead things live? Solely by the magic of one simple process: *by making them human,* and so bringing them home (by the touch of kindred) to the intuitive comprehension and sympathy of our minds. How

LECT. II.

else can anything in heaven or earth be brought home to us, or be put in communion with us, than by making it *human?*[1] Take, for instance, the arrow-headed strokes on an undeciphered ASSYRIAN tablet. They can, of course, be numbered, be measured, be copied, be compared. But meanwhile all is dark, dumb, devoid of interest, a series of hard, dead lines. But, in a moment perhaps, certain sequences dawn out into a human name: the light then grows apace: the stone becomes vocal, historical: and ere long, in known terms of man's life and man's way of acting and thinking, a buried and forgotten race becomes intelligible and alive again to commune with their brother men.[2] Precisely in the same

[1] The same thought seems to have occurred to the perverted mind of Schopenhauer. "Unsere Bewunderung der unendlichen Vollkommenheit und Zweckmässigkeit in den Werken der Natur beruht im Grunde darauf, dass wir sie im Sinn unserer Werke betrachten."—(*Wille in der Natur*, p. 55.) But from want of any *faith* in the relative veracity of our conceptions, "what might have been for his wealth becomes to him an occasion of falling;" and refusing (as it were) to see with the aids assigned for seeing, he is of course unable to see anything at all. Floundering in a similar abyss of hopeless scepticism as to the trustworthiness of our faculties, one man believes in "transubstantiation," while another cries that "the heavens declare the glory" of no one beyond Kepler and Copernicus.—(*Cf.* Strauss, *A. und N. Glaube*, p. 216.)

[2] See the deeply interesting exhumation of Hittite history described in Sayce's *Fresh Light from the Ancient Monuments*, Religious Tract Society, 1884.

way, in Geology, the testimony of the rocks to ancient forms of animal life, and to the long history of our planet, dawned out upon the last generation. At first the note-books of observers were filled with dead intellectual facts, to which no rational meaning could be given. But at last the imagination awoke to clothe it all in human forms and to give it living touch with the human mind. And then dead rocks became "strata," as though it were of human masonry; slant surfaces became "tilted," as though with some giant's upheaval; crushed and shattered skeletons were repaired, and a kind of human "life" was imagined back into them, like the life which we feel impelled to attribute to the kindred animals around us. In short, Geology became possible solely by reducing into terms of our own inward experience the outside facts of dead Nature, and by clothing non-human phenomena with a human meaning.[1] Once more,

[1] First attempts, in science as well as elsewhere, will often provoke a smile. Thus the earliest effort to "humanise" the occurrence of shells on mountain heights was to suppose them floated there, like Noah's ark, by the deluge. Then came Voltaire's celebrated attempt to discredit the deluge by supposing the shells dropped by pilgrims from the East. Then the jocose side of human nature was utilised by attributing the shells to a freak or "practical joke" of Nature. Lastly, the truth began to dawn.—(See Lyell, *Principles of Geology*, 7th edition, p. 56: or Miss Buckley's *Short History of Natural Science*, p. 214.)

in Astronomy, what caused NEWTON to start from his desk in such a state of mental agitation that his trembling fingers refused to draw his long-accumulated piles of dumb and senseless figures out to their now foreseen conclusion? It was simply that a *human* meaning had suddenly dawned upon the arithmetical chaos and had transformed it into Cosmos; that the notion of a mutual drawing together as *men* know the sensation, and in proportion to mass and distance as *men* weigh and measure such things, had seized (like resurrection) upon the senseless facts. The Solar System, in short, had abruptly become *intelligible*, simply because it had (in a way) become *human*.

Such illustrations might be multiplied to any extent that the argument might require, and proofs might be drawn from every department of physical science.[1] But the samples now given

---

[1] No more striking instance of the success which attends this "humanising" of Nature could be found than is presented in a charming little book lately published by Mr. Taylor, and entitled (oddly enough) *The Sagacity and Morality of Plants*. Writers of a less popular kind often think it necessary to pause occasionally, when using similar language, and to deprecate being taken *au sérieux*. But they are obliged to use such language, nevertheless, on every page if they would be either interesting or intelligible. Even Vignoli, who would degrade this action of the fancy to a mere bestial instinct derived from our ape-like ancestors, and who glorifies Science as the "depersonification of

are probably sufficient to carry conviction to every thoughtful mind, and to establish the axiom that without "anthropomorphism" every science remains barren, and its results are inconceivable to our minds.

(2.) And if so, we must now gird up our attention and make an effort to ascend from these lower ranges of study to that loftiest pinnacle of all earthly thinking to which Religion invites us. For to this height, too, the universal principle we are now in possession of will accompany us, and will render our course intelligible and secure. It will show us how to deal even with that fundamental question which lies at the

myth," complains that scientific men "regard 'laws' as substantial entities."—(*Myth and Science*, Intern. series, 1882, p. 195.) The fact is, they cannot help it. And though Plato, long ago, led the way in describing "the processes of measuring and counting and weighing, as aids towards dispelling these tricks of fancy"—(*Republic*, English trans., p. 602); yet even the prosaic Baxter allows "it must be a point of spiritual prudence to call in [pictorial] sense to our assistance"—(*Saints' Rest*, p. 251); while Renan declares that art "a, de nos jours, une fonction religieuse supérieure à celle du théologien"— (*Études*, p. 430), and Herbert Spencer, confessing that "very likely there will ever remain a need to give shape to that indefinite sense of an ultimate existence which forms the basis of our intelligence," unnecessarily adds, "We shall not err in doing this, so long as we treat every notion we thus form as merely a symbol, utterly without resemblance to that for which it stands." —(*First Principles*, p. 112.) Why should we thus go out of our way consciously to spoil, for ourselves and for others, the power of the symbol to suggest to us that of which it is the symbol?

D

LECT. II.

bottom of all Theology and determines its whole course—the question of the existence and attributes of God. Of course, if there be no GOD theology comes to an end, and all our religion is vain. For we cannot make up our minds, with Dr. Büchner and the ancient Phœnicians, to worship heat: nor can we seriously pretend, with the Positivists, to adore abstract Humanity. No doubt, we are grateful to mankind for all their good work in clearing forests, destroying monsters, and enduring innumerable sanguinary conflicts to secure the survival of ourselves upon these fair fields of earth. But science discloses to us interminable periods of time before Humanity existed at all. And far behind Hercules and Cecrops, and the whole calendar of primæval benefactors to society, there stretch out enormous spaces wherein Nature alone, without man, held sway, and where accordingly the Christian and the Positivist part company. For what is a "religion" worth which cannot see behind the advent of Man upon the Globe; which cannot idealise and personify the Universal Force itself; and cannot even echo such old-world thoughts as that "man is the measure of all things," and that human reason (λόγος) sits at the right hand of Cosmic power, except by abolishing the idea of God and bidding us worship Man?

No: seriously doubt the existence of God, and religion—in any rational sense of the word—must come to an end. The poetry of the world is then gone: and prose reigns supreme. All hope of idealising Nature's unity, and of bringing it home in human attributes to our human imagination, is at an end. Frittered into a multitude of details, "the wood cannot be seen for the trees:" the city cannot be grasped because of its houses: the Almighty cannot be discerned because of His works. "And then" (as an eloquent writer has lately described it) "theories are rejected one by one; the great books are returned sadly to their shelves: and at length conflicting truths, like the beams of light in the laboratory-experiment, combine to make total darkness in the mind."[1] Yes—says an Atheist who had passed through

---

[1] Drummond, *Natural Law in the Spiritual World*, 7th edition, p. 237. This singular and eloquent book has attained a great popularity; but every thoughtful reader of its laboured argumentation feels tempted to exclaim, as he approaches the ultimate issue—"Nascetur ridiculus mus." What! only those immortal who are "converted," in the Presbyterian sense of the word! It is perfectly easy to make Scripture texts seem to countenance any theory whatever—even the Anglo-Israel craze. And, as the earliest Latin Father pointed out 1700 years ago, "Nihil proficit congressio Scripturarum nisi plane ut aut *stomachi* quis incat eversionem, aut *cerebri*." [A warfare of Scripture-texts sends a man either off his head or off his temper.] (Tertullian, *Præscrip.*, § 16.) In fact, "Trägt der heutige Leser ebensoviel in Sie hinein, als er aus Ihr entnimmt."—(Strauss, *Alte und Neue Glaube*, 4th edition, p. 301.)

LECT. II.

all these dismal experiences—"we have lived to see the sun shine out of an empty heaven, to light up a soul-less earth: we have felt with utter loneliness, that the Great Companion is dead."[1]

Is there, then, a God; or is there not? Let us first inquire why, on a sudden, in these days, such a question as this should press seriously for an answer? It is not necessary on the present occasion to dwell on the prevalence of one "obstacle to belief" which, if it is not founded on some deeper perplexity, is hardly worthy of serious mention,—I mean, impatience aroused by the inadequate language about God habitually employed by many Christian teachers. All our language upon such a subject must, surely, be utterly inadequate. And, in addressing the ignorant and childlike, there is absolute necessity for adapting thought and language to their needs.[2]

---

[1] Prof. Clifford, *Essays*, ii., 247.

[2] At the same time, I must honestly confess that I think much of the language which religious people use—amid the culture and knowledge of the present day—about Almighty God, is highly imprudent and almost unpardonable. It is of the first necessity, at the present day, that Christian teachers should expand and elevate their whole conception of what the divine agency in the universe is like. Whatever their language may be, or whatever the symbols they habitually employ, their ideas about God should soar above—not sink below—those of the ordinary students and admirers of Nature; and they should sometimes allow it to be seen that such is the case. To be

Nor can I think worthy of much attention another obstacle which, however real and solid, is not peculiar to Christianity nor characteristic of the present day,—I mean the inexplicable mystery of the existence of evil. Some philosophers have indeed persuaded themselves that the theory of "Evolution" explains away this mystery. They hold that, since we partly see how conflict and death issue in the improvement of the world, therefore suffering and degradation are sufficiently

circumscribed, for instance, in thinking about the supreme adorable Power that determines all things by mere analogies derived from Oriental despotisms—such as we read of in Herodotus or the Book of Esther—is not only contrary to the Christian faith, as expressed in the Athanasian Creed, but is contrary to common sense and common prudence. Why should we give occasion to the enemies of God to blaspheme? The Creator is represented, says Haeckel, as "an almighty man who plans and constructs a variety of toys."—(*History of Creation*, i., p. 66.) "Voltaire," says Dr. Büchner, "taught that 'Si Dieu n'existait pas, il faut [for political reasons] l'inventer;' and Robespierre, with great pomp restored the Supreme Being, precisely as one sets up or dethrones an earthly king. "Gott spielt dabei die Rolle eines Popanzes oder Polizei-büttels, welcher stets mit aufgehobener Ruthe vor den Menchen steht und ihnen wie bösen Kindern droht: Wenn ihr nicht artig seyd, so werde Ich euch an mich denken lehren!"—(*Der Gottes-begriff*, 1874, p. 56.) In another work, criticising certain notions about Pantheism pointing to Revolution and Theism to Absolute Monarchy, he makes a touching appeal to the Christian clergy: "We should believe in the possibility of a peaceful issue, if it were possible for the clergy and for statesmen, instead of following their present ways, to take an intermediate course between these extremes." —(*Science and Nature*, French trans., i. 15.)

accounted for; and, whether all be for the best or not, that we at least know the reason why we are so miserable. The solution of the enigma (if it be a solution) is welcome to Christians, so far as it goes; for, to that extent, it aids them to justify the ways of God towards men and towards the other creatures that are sensitive of pain. But, in point of fact, it leaves the difficulty precisely where it was before. It explains indeed how a great many evils are the outcome of certain laws—laws of "struggle for existence," of "sexual selection," of "survival of the fittest"—but it in no way explains how or why such laws of suffering and waste ever came to be imposed upon the universe. To that insoluble question the reason of man has but two possible modes of reply. One is, the despair and pessimism of Schopenhauer—who holds (to use popular language) that the world was created by the devil. The other is, the belief and hope of St. Paul—who trusts, in spite of many perplexities, that all things are sustained and governed by God, who is Love. In short, St. Paul relegates us, once more, to Faith —to a moral solution of obstinate intellectual difficulties—as the only outlet to confidence and peace that is open to faculties so limited as ours; and St. John's position is anticipated, that there is only one way of mastering the world and surmounting its obstacles, and that is by the ethical intuitions of a well-trained conscience.[1]

Meanwhile, there is undoubtedly one real obstacle to the acceptance of a Christian belief in God, which has in our day assumed a large and menacing aspect. It is the philosophy of Materialism. On not a few minds of the highest order—especially among those who have given themselves with a noble self-devotion to the study of Nature—a strong suspicion of the all-

---

[1] This necessity of "Faith," *i.e.* of moral serenity and stability, as a preliminary to intellectual knowledge—though denied by hard thinkers like Professor Clifford—(*Essays*, ii. 219), was strongly felt by able men like Clement of Alexandria (*Strom.*, vii. p. 732), Origen (*c. Celsum*, i. 11), and Anselm (*Cur Deus Homo*, i. 2), who states the matter tersely, thus : "Credo ut intelligam." He means, there is a certain atmosphere, a certain climate, which is essential—in Theology, as in every other branch of knowledge—to productiveness. "We are warned by Professor Ramsay that a long process of geological education is required to realise the conception 'of denudation.'"—(*Scepticism in Geology*, 2nd edition, 1878, p. 87.) "At first the mind refuses to take in revealed facts : but by degrees the steady contemplation of these facts so strengthens and expands the intellectual powers, that where truth once could not find an entrance, it eventually finds a home."—(Professor Tyndall, *Lecture at Royal Institution*, June 9, 1876.) "Till we accept the *faiths* which our faculties postulate, we can never *know* even the sensible world ; and when we accept them, we shall know much more."—(J. Martineau, in *Contemporary Review*, March, 1876.) "It is the inclination and tendency of the heart which finally determines the opinions of the mind."—(Luthardt, *Fundamental Truths of Christianity*, English trans., p. 25.)

sufficiency of "matter" to explain the universe has laid a powerful hold. It is seen that all phenomena are, in some way, associated with matter: it is believed that matter, in an attenuated form, fills all space, and that across a vacuum no message of any kind can reach us: and it is alleged that, apart from the aid of certain highly composite molecules of matter, neither consciousness nor thought is known to exist. Hence the im-material is confounded with the non-existent. "Apart from matter, there is no such thing as force, or movement, or tension, or resistance."[1] "The profession of a materialist faith is, at the present day, no mere presentiment or prophecy; but the result of a deeply-rooted conviction."[2] "The theologians have their dogmas; and we have ours. They are these: (*a*) matter has existed from eternity; (*b*) out of this the world has formed itself; (*c*) from its inherent qualities the changeless laws have emanated by which the world is maintained. Nowhere do we find any place for God, . . . your 'God' is nothing else than a personification of *force*."[3]

---

[1] Büchner, *Light and Life*, French trans., p. 124.
[2] Moleschott, *Circulation of Life*, French trans., ii., p. 57.
[3] Hartmann, *God and Science*, ii., p. 72; cf. "*Darwinism*," pp. 22 and 14.

But observe, we have there, in that last word, what Aristotle would call a μετάβασις εἰς ἄλλο γένος: in other words, we have that fruitful parent of all mystification and fallacy, the unnoticed *substitution of a new idea* for the one originally under discussion. "Matter" certainly is *one* thing; and "materialism" ought to mean the acceptance of matter as a sufficient explanation of all phenomena in heaven and earth. But "matter" and "force" surely are *two* things, not one thing. For nobody would undertake to maintain that a substance and the various qualities—often fugitive and successive—which attach to the substance, are absolutely one and indistinguishable. No one would say that iron and the force which expanded and coloured and liquefied it, were one and the same thing. No one would assert that an oratorio was identical with so many pages of music and so many yards of catgut and brass-tubing. Nor can this fatal objection be evaded by pleading that the word "matter" has nowadays assumed a wider meaning; and that it now embraces all the "forces," latent or active, which from age to age it may evolve. For this only pushes the question a stage further back; the intellect at once busies itself to analyse this still more wonderful "matter" again into its component parts: viz. (1) substance, (2) qualities;

and so the Dualism—which was conjured so deftly away—is instantly restored. It were better, therefore, to retain the old words; to say that matter is one thing and force another thing; to believe, with Mr. Spencer, that there is "a *power* which the Universe manifests to us";[1] and to hold, with Dr. Büchner, that "all the way-posts point to one goal—the unity of matter, the unity of force."[2] And if this Dualism—which first sums up all the sixty-three elements into one word "*matter*," and then all the eight forms of motion into one word "*force*" —be an accepted fact, then the Atheist (it seems) should come over to our side. For (as Mr. Bradlaugh says), "It is necessary that every form of *Dualism* should be rejected. . . . It is only by reaching *unity* that we can have a reasonable conclusion. . . . Either Atheism or Theism must be the true doctrine of the Universe."[3] Certainly: the mind cannot rest until it attains the idea of unity. The ascertained *Duality*, therefore, of matter and of force must needs find its point of unity a stage higher still; and so we are led to the only further point in which these and all other lines converge in absolute unity—the ultimate idea of GOD. *Theism*, therefore, and not

---

[1] Spencer, *First Principles*, p. 46.
[2] *Light and Life*, p. 73.   [3] *Plea for Atheism*, p. 23.

Atheism, alone satisfies the human mind, and turns out to be the true theory of the universe.

(3.) But why (it may be asked) should that only which satisfies the *human mind* be regarded as true; and that which leaves it dissatisfied and restless be rejected as false? This (as everybody knows) is the standing question of Philosophy. And it were well that it should nowadays be answered out of hand, and be finally laid at rest. For, after all that has been written and thought and said for ages upon the subject, there really can no longer be any reasonable doubt about the answer, nor any hesitation in affirming plainly, that *the human mind has nothing whatever to do with absolute and outside truth:* that it is but a mirror,[1] constructed to image forth the universe in a manner impressive and useful and delightful to us; and that its presentment, therefore, is *relative,* not absolute, truth. And, since we can never get behind ourselves, cannot see except with the eye, nor think except with the brain, it

---

[1] "Uhlich, in a pamphlet penetrated by the noblest feeling for truth, calls religion 'the science of sciences;' he explains truth as 'the reflection of reality, of the real world with its things and forces, laws and processes, in the soul of man.'"—(Lange, *History of Materialism,* iii., p. 284.) "The human mind is always, in some degree, a reflecting surface (as it were) for the verities of the unseen and eternal world."—(Duke of Argyll, *Unity of Nature,* 1884, p. 122.)

is obvious that the very first and most essential act in all our mental work must be (as was before pointed out) an act of pure FAITH—*faith* in the sufficiency of our faculties, *faith* in the approximate veracity (for all practical purposes) of our mental mirror, *faith* in the gift we possess of interpreting all things in terms of our own mind, complete in its triple functions of INTELLECT, IMAGINATION, and CONSCIENCE.

Any one can test the reasonableness of this Faith for himself. Take any subject you please, and think it out. Reflect, for instance, on the law of gravitation: and first try to disbelieve the *intellectual* veracity of such a notion as "the square of the distance"—instantly Newton's discovery tumbles into ruins, and chaos is reinstated in our conception of the universe. Disbelieve next (as one might easily do, if cynically disposed) the *imaginative* picture of two great globes "pulling at" each other, or "being weighed" against each other, or as escaping a fatal shock by centrifugal flight—instantly you are back among columns of dead figures again, and your supposed brilliant acquisition becomes dust and ciphers in your hands. Or throw scorn, lastly, on the *moral* facet of your mental mirror; smile sadly away any notion it may suggest of a good and serious "purpose" in all this reign of law; let haphazard be king; or, worse, let malignity be supposed to have set all things in motion, and "gravitation" to be nothing better than an accursed clockwork set going for the production of the utmost possible confusion, misery, and ruin—and then, once more, Newton's splendid discovery collapses. It is rejected by the common-sense of mankind. For men refuse with healthy intuition to see in this wonderful universe either a contemptible work of blind chance or a hideous reign of infinite and almighty malice. "Rather (say they) we will wait for further information; and meanwhile, 'in patience possess we our souls.'"

Thus it appears that even within the narrow illuminated zone within which real knowledge can be attained, and where Science is most at home, FAITH in the veracity of our mental faculties—however limited and relative all their knowledge may be—is the one essential condition of success. How much more, when we look forth at either frontier of clear consciousness into the darkness and mystery beyond! For, as Krishna says in the ancient Hindu poem, "All things which exist are invisible in their primal state, visible in their intermediate state, and again invisible in their final state."[1] And, as Mr. Spencer says to-day, "Alike in the external and the internal worlds,

[1] Thomson's *Bhagavat-gita*, p. 13.

LECT. II.

the man of science finds himself in the midst of perpetual changes, of which he can discover neither the beginning nor the end."[1] Everywhere, then, we are met by the imperative necessity of Faith—and most of all when we contemplate that pictured sheet (as it were) which our mind presents to us as the boundary of our conscious knowledge, whereon is projected a brief foreshortened summary, for practical religious purposes, of the great unknown which lies beyond. When, therefore, on that pictured screen we recognise, with the vast majority of mankind, the solemn, awful figure of an unknown *Power*, one and harmonious behind all ceaseless play of change; when we trace there the lineaments of an unfathomable *Wisdom*, guiding, evolving, and balancing all that exists; and when we read there a firm, calm *Will*, reaching ends by certain selected ways and steadily evolving the more perfect from the less perfect, order out of chaos, and good out of evil; we are not to be deterred by any foolish fear of "anthropomorphism" from accepting, here too, with confidence such conceptions as the human imagination is irresistibly impelled to form.[2] We combine the triple impression

---

[1] Spencer, *First Principles*, p. 66.

[2] Τὰ εἴδη τῶν θεῶν ἀφομοιοῦσιν ἑαυτοῖς οἱ ἄνθρωποι.—(Arist. *Polit.*, i., 2.) "If there be a God at all, it is manifest to

made upon us into a superior unity. And, falling low in adoration, we confess, in some stammering form of utterly inadequate human speech, the mysterious presence of GOD.

Let him that *can* live without any such awakened consciousness of God, let him that *can* say, "I know not what you mean by God: I am without the idea of God," try to live his life worthily that way.[1] The animals around him do the same; living contentedly between their barriers of sense; "materialists" according to their lights. But let him acknowledge that most human beings (at any rate) are compelled by the very constitution of their minds to go further, and to ask who or what is that power which—from within or from without—has developed matter to its present marvellous complexity, so that (as Darwin says) "we stand in awe before the mystery of life."[2]

Or again, if any philosopher *can* stop with the bare idea of power, in his researches into the origin of things, and can exclaim (with the buoyant self-confidence of a Büchner), "without object,

every one who reflects, that there is no possible method of describing His deeds or His nature, except that of adopting language appropriate to man."—(Bishop Goodwin, *Walks*, &c., p. 293.)

[1] Bradlaugh, *Plea for Atheism*, p. 4.
[2] *Cross-fertilisation in Plants*, p. 458.

without cause, Eternity rolls round upon itself, though the human spirit recoils before so simple a solution of the world's great enigma,"[1]—let him do so. Only let him remember that the very same imaginative faculty which has conceived—from interior muscular sensations—the idea of "force," ought from innumerable indications of what we feel as purpose and contrivance to infer also a cosmic attribute of "wisdom."

Or again, if any one *can* be content with a discovery of power and wisdom only, be it so; and let him guard himself, with what courage he may, against the suspicion that this awful cosmic POWER has aims which he can in no way forecast, and that this awful WISDOM may possibly be a vast malignant cunning. But let him know that to the vast majority of mankind such a suspicion that the devil may be sitting at the world's helm is positively intolerable and even ludicrous; and that, when "*improvement*" seems the guiding idea in all selection and all evolution, when "*enhanced intelligence*" seems the purpose of all cerebral change, and when "*nobility of character*," seems the object aimed at by such evil in the world as we can understand at all, it is impossible to persuade them that GOODNESS is not, along with power and wisdom, a characteristic of the Spirit

[1] *Light and Life*, French trans., p. 241.

that guides the universe. And since wisdom and goodness cannot, consistently with any sane use of our human faculties, be assigned to an unconscious being—since every impulse of our nature, every fresh discovery of our own impotence, every new revelation of the wonder of the universe, all compel us to look up to the world-power with awe, and forbid us to look down upon it with airs of superiority; and since our human brain (the only organ we have for thinking purposes) will not let us believe that an aërolite "falling down from Jupiter," with its blind physical momentum, nor yet an Assyrian bull or an Egyptian crocodile, with their headlong brutal instincts, form any sufficient type of the energy that sways the universe,[1]—we seem driven by the very constitution of our faculties to attribute to that majestic energy full *consciousness* of what it does, or perhaps something far higher than "consciousness," of which our human brain-power is but a distant reflection and a type.[2]

---

[1] "Ein Unbewusstes . . . eine blinde Naturkraft . . . Auf die Höhe (!) dieses Standpunkts hat uns die neuere Naturforschung in Darwin geführt."—(Strauss, *Alte und neue Glaube*, p. 219.)

[2] "Is it not just possible that there is a mode of being as much transcending Intelligence and Will, as these transcend mechanical motion? It is true we are totally unable to conceive any such higher mode of being. But this is not a reason for questioning its existence."—(Spencer, *First Principles*, p. 108.)

And if so, we have at last reached, in this grand combination of attributes, the Christian conception of GOD. And in reaching it, we have passed the line at which mere speculation merges into Religion. For such a Being has assumed (what Christians mean by) "personality." In other words, intercommunion has now become possible: we can approach, we can worship, we can love: the thing we call "prayer" begins to suggest itself: the springs of hope and fear are touched: and amid all the baffling complexity, and sometimes terror, of the surrounding cosmos our earthly life may now be passed in filial serenity and confidence. We may henceforth feel that we walk with a divine companion, and that the irresistible world-power has become to us as a personal friend and (in touching anthropomorphic phrase) "our Father which is in Heaven."

LECTURE III.

CREATION.

GEN. i. 1: "In the beginning God created the heavens and the earth."

IN the last lecture an attempt was made to establish the position, that—since all truth, without any exception, if it is to come home to us and be conceivable by us, must be imaged upon the retina (as it were) of our minds in some kindred and anthropomorphic way—it follows inevitably that the majestic undivided Power, which the universe as a whole reveals to us, can only be rationally conceived in the same manner. The Deity, in short, can only be thought of by us in terms of the human mind. And we saw that this innocent—nay, unavoidable—anthropomorphism carries with it the triple idea of a transcendent Power, Wisdom, and Goodness: which three qualities, combined and welded together in

LECT. III.

a substantial unity, form the Christian conception of GOD.

We must now advance a step further; and the next problem must be faced, which presents itself in reflecting upon the universe as a whole. It is that problem of the Divine causation of all things which is popularly expressed by the word "Creation." The Christian doctrine on this subject is perfectly clear and positive. It affirms that God created and sustains Nature; or, in other words, that mind stands first in the order of thought, and not matter. For, of the two, one must be first. We cannot rest in a dualism. Everything points to a unity in Nature. When, therefore, our own experience presents us with the striking contrast between a corpse and a living man; when our irresistible intuitions compel us to assign a quite infinite superiority to that conscious life (mind) which alone differentiates the man from the corpse; and when all the sciences at present affirm that no corpse, or matter of any kind, is able to generate life—even in its lowest degree—while life (on the contrary) seizes and transforms matter, and conscious-life (or "mind") transfigures the whole face of the globe; the inference seems irresistible that mind predominates over matter. And so, if the question be raised, which of the two was antecedent, in order of time and in order of causation, the answer given by Christianity is the only one consonant to reason: viz., that *in the universe, as a whole, mind was first and was the cause of matter.* In other words, " In the beginning GOD created the heavens and the earth." This text, then, is a brief, pictorial, and popular way of stating a profound truth. Subtle language is not for the populace. Yet the whole brotherhood of mankind is interested in these problems and asks these questions. What would a teacher be worth who could not express his answer in terms intelligible to his pupil?

(1.) It seems strange, therefore, that cultivated and scientific men should be found so thoughtless or so ignorant of mankind as to declaim against the Church's continued use of that simple picture-language which, in Genesis, has proved itself, for ages, the most efficient "teacher of babes" that could possibly have been found. For it has laid firmly down, in all the more civilised countries of the globe, the two first stepping-stones to any sound physical knowledge: (1) The essential unity which lies at the bottom of all things; (2) that most singular anticipation of the truth, viz., the process of Creation by stages, in ever-ascending order, and with rest (for the present) in the appearance of man. It seems strange indeed, and not a little childish, that great philosophers should go out of their way to have a fling at this picture-book for the unlearned; and parodying (as is often said) the noble poetry of the Bible into so much bald prose, should gravely take to pieces (what the *Replies to "Essays and Reviews"* called) "this Psalm of the Divine Creation," and should try to rob the people of so precious and suitable a lesson book.

Yet this surprising folly is committed every day. Thus Dr. Hartmann puts on airs of scorn, and says, "We children of the newer time can no longer make the mystery of Creation consist—like the gross conception of former days—in the hardened clay, the breath divine, and so forth."[1] Dr. Moleschott goes further. He thinks the idea of "Creation" nonsense, and he naïvely tells us why: "When Liebig begins to talk of the laws of Nature and, in the same breath, of a Creator, he ceases to be intelligible; for the laws of Nature are an expression of the most rigorous necessity—and necessity excludes Creation."[2] We will deal with that presently. But meanwhile we may amuse ourselves with the sorry mirth of a favourite American orator, who describes how "a supreme being took some nothing and made

---

[1] *Darwinisme*, 3rd edition, p. 24.
[2] *Circulation de la Vie*, p. 6.

a world and one man;" and with the curious impatience of even Mr. Herbert Spencer, who is indignant with the "carpenter theory" of Creation.[1] Yet this admirable writer candidly confesses on another page that " The gross body of dogmas, traditions, and rites [in short, the whole apparatus of the Church] renders the truth more appreciable to lower perceptions: they serve to make real and influential over men that which would else be unreal and uninfluential."[2] While a shrewd thinker, Professor Huxley, clearly sees the common sense of the matter, and exposes the absurdity of seriously assaulting a man of straw, or of "discussing a view which no one upholds."[3] Let, therefore, irritable philosophers like Vignoli proclaim a crusade against all use of myth and picture-language for the unlearned, if they think it worthy of their cause to do so.[4] The Christian Church holds it both more rational and more charitable "not to destroy, but to fulfil;" to fill out the whole framework, and to breathe into it a fuller meaning; and not passionately to break the imperfect mirror, but to purify and improve it. For (as Professor Tyndall admirably says) even "the study of Natural Science goes hand-in-hand with the culture of the Imagination. . . .

---

[1] *First Principles*, p. 113. [2] *First Principles*, p. 121.
[3] *The Crayfish*, p. 319. [4] *Myth and Science*, p. 429.

LECT. III.

We picture atoms and molecules and vibrations and waves, which eye has never seen nor ear heard, and which can only be discerned by the Imagination."[1] Yes; the "culture" of the Imagination, not its repudiation; the diligent attempt to polish that inward mirror, and to correct it from stains that blur and unevennesses that distort its representations—that is the true work to be done for mankind. And in proportion as that is successfully accomplished, the artificial helps of myth legend and symbolism can, without fatal mischief, be replaced by a personal and independent power of reflecting the universe and of seeing its real meaning by direct intuition. To this high perfection it is that Christianity invites us all.

(2.) But there is a second, and a far more serious, objection raised against the Christian doctrine of Creation: it is the objection which emblazons on its banner the now familiar word "Evolution." For this favourite theory is supposed, in some quarters, to stand in flagrant contradiction to the idea of a Divine creation.[2] But since the hypothesis of Evolution is nothing else than an attempt to explain *how* the heavens and the earth were created, leaving the statement quite untouched that they *were* created, it is

---

[1] *Radiation* (1865), p. 60.
[2] "Physicus," *Theism*, p. 41.

difficult to see how the two notions can come into collision with one another. The one simply takes up the story where the other leaves it off. And we have only to place them end to end, thus: "From God all things took their origin; and by successive stages of evolution He made them to become what they now are:" in order to see quite clearly how the ancient and the modern statements are merely one line prolonged. We may, therefore, decline to argue (as is frequently done) that the Evolution theory remains at present in a very precarious condition—though the allegation is true. For I hold it quite unworthy of Christians to show any slight, or even to accord a reluctant acceptance, to the only theory of Creation which has hitherto thrown any light on this mysterious subject. For it is not light, it is darkness, to say (with the ancient sages) "water is the first principle of all things," or "fire is the first principle," or "all things came out of a cosmic egg," or "the world came forth by an oversight while Brahma slept." Nor is it sufficient to assert, with the ancient Hebrews, that "Jehovah spake the word and all things were made." The question now raised by Science is the further question, "What, more precisely, did Jehovah speak? What were the laws which proceeded out of His mouth?"

And if it should be ascertained—as it promises to be—that the creative laws, which have produced all this marvellous complexity we find around us, were the same on a vast scale as those which we see with our own eyes at work on the small scale; if it should appear that births, not startling apparitions, have throughout been God's method; that His laws have always been laws of growth (as we know it in the crystal, the plant, the animal), not of abrupt finality; and that steadfast continuity of plan has characterised creation, not a fitful and feeble caprice; surely all these discoveries come home to us as, in the highest sense, human, rational, intelligible. The conception of the primal creative "word" is now expanded into that of a majestic stream of legislation, permeating and controlling all things; the creative "fiat" is rescued from humiliating comparison with a magician's potent spell; and the statement becomes for the first time clear and comprehensible, that "by the WORD—the Logos, or intelligible reason—of God all things, in heaven and earth, were made."

(3.) But there is a third objection raised against the Christian doctrine of Creation. And this the Church refuses to treat so lightly. On the contrary, she firmly condemns it as un-human, irrational, immoral. It is that obstacle put forward by Dr. Moleschott in the passage already quoted: "The laws of Nature are the expression of the most rigorous *necessity*—and necessity excludes creation." He means, I presume, that all things are as they are by a rigid and irresistible fate; that fate sweeps onwards gyrating nebulæ, suns, comets, planets, geological formations, the ever-growing complexity of chemical molecules, the mutual adaptation between insects and plants, the ever-multiplying varieties of animal life, and all the fretful, feverish activities of man upon this globe, in one blind, inexorable torrent of necessity—beginning (as Dr. Büchner puts it) nowhere and ending nowhere, without purpose, without cause, without intelligence.[1] It is indeed a grand, Titanic conception; heathen, sombre, awful; dark as Erebus, solemn as some great drama of Æschylus, a real Tragedy of the Universe; extinguishing all hope, suppressive of all energy, derisive of all freedom, a *reductio ad absurdum* of all human responsibility, and a sentence (as it were) to a dumb and passive endurance of involuntary servitude for life for the whole human race.

Yet there are doubtless some indications which (at first sight) point that way. In the first place

[1] *Light and Life*, French trans., p. 241.

LECT. III.

a very little serious thought, as he paces homewards beneath a star-lit sky, is sufficient to send any man upon his knees in awe and utter self-abasement. Who are we, that have just left perhaps some highly important public meeting, that have risen in our place in Parliament, that have finished our poem, painted our great picture of the season, or drawn to its result some profound calculation which is to revolutionise the world of science? We are dust, we are motes in the sunbeam, we are bubbles carried down the foaming rapids of Niagara. With vast and majestic force, with speed and momentum to which the tranquil aspect of things forms an irrisive veil, we and all our works are being hurled through space, amid a dance of giant suns and flaming comets, at which one's heart stands still. At 60,000 miles an hour this tiny spray-drop we call "the earth" is speeding on; at 20,000 miles an hour (it is believed) the huge solar system itself is advancing into new and untried spaces; while our neighbour Sirius is calculated to be dashing from us at a speed of 118,000 miles an hour, and the nearest star in Cygnus is flashing along at 140,000 miles an hour.[1]

---

[1] Proctor, *Astronomical Essays*, p. 270; ditto, *The Study of Nature*, in *Fraser's Magazine*, September, 1871. Cf. Herschel, *Astronomy*, p. 311.

The energy of the universe is, indeed, portentous. Should the earth suddenly stand still, the heat generated (as in an arrested bullet) would rise to 11,000°; and every terrestrial thing would become a wreath of vapour.¹ One single lightning-spark (the merest trifle) has been measured; its flash was ten and a half miles long: another, from immediately overhead, struck down a man three miles away. Aërolites come rushing furiously into our upper atmosphere, and in 1872 Professor Secchi counted 14,000 of them in three hours. One such mass fell unconsumed, and is now in Paris; it weighs twelve hundredweight. Another, in 1872, fell in America; it broke a tree, killed a man, and then buried itself two feet in the hard frozen ground.² Yet, balloonists tell us, when you rise 2,600 feet above this noisy earth all is placid, deep, unbroken silence.³ The busy hum of millions of insects is unheard; the cattle upon a thousand hills vanish into points; the city roar is reduced to zero; the clashing of the battle is noiseless; the earthquake ruins a metropolis and is unperceived; while man and all his works,

LECT. III.

---

[1] Somerville, *Molecular Science*, i. 27. Reis, *Le Soleil*, 1869, puts it at a much higher figure. See also Sir Edm. Beckett, *Origin of the Laws of Nature*, p. 35.

[2] *Nature*, 1880, p. 64; cf. Flammarion, *The Atmosphere*, pp. 179, 479. Hartwig, *Subterranean World*, p. 347.

[3] Glaisher, *Travels in the Air*, p. 364.

LECT. III.

and the great planet on which he lives and frets and dies, seem borne along by a silent, irresistible, inexorable force. You may call it "fate," if you please: but you are not obliged to call it "fate." There is quite another theory, a message of good news to man, which peremptorily forbids him so to call it, and rather cheers and animates him with a summons to arouse his moral force and to trust a better hope than that. It bids him, in short, frankly to *believe* (how can he possibly *prove* such a thing by algebra or logic?) that the power which moves all this tremendous mechanism is not a frightful, blind, and headlong "fate," but a merciful and living GOD. "Why" (say you) "should he believe it?" Because this belief is alone *rational*, and mirrors definitely and completely the experiences of his own inner nature: while the other conception—grand and sombre though it be, like a monstrous Hindoo temple—is irrational, contradicts inward experience, and draws its inspiration from a defective observation of human consciousness instead of a complete observation. Suppose that, granting personal consciousness to be the key to all the great world's movements, we should argue from our bony framework alone, and should say, "These things lie where they are put: they are passive: they are pulled by ligaments; the ligaments are shortened by muscles;

the muscles are shrunk by a nerve. All is mechanism; all is a chain of necessity. My passive frame, therefore, explains to me the Universe." Is it not clear that such a mere anatomist's view of things would be a very imperfect and partial one? No: we must summon the Biologist into the field. And then we shall hear, if he be Professor Huxley, a confession that the power of *volition* " counts for something ; "[1] in short, that you must not, with a spot, shut off the Will from your microscopic investigation. And then, *all* things (not *some* things) considered, this fact of a WILL, of which we are more immediately and intuitively conscious than of anything else in the whole universe,[2] stands out as the leading fact in our inner world; and therefore supplies (as it seems meant to do) the most rational and

---

[1] Huxley, *Lay Sermons;* cf. Graham, *Creed of Science*, 1881, p. 146 : " In spite of the speculative conclusion that the will is not a free causal agency, is there not the equally clear practical conviction that man *can* control the course of his life and actions to some considerable degree? I think we must admit it." Bersier, *Sermons*, iv. 109 : " Chacun de vos actes est la contradiction la plus frappante apportée à votre système. Vous ne pouvez modifier la Nature ; et à chaque instant vous la modifiez."

[2] So the Duke of Argyll, *Unity of Nature*, 1884, p. 115 : "We know the operations of our own minds with a fulness and reality which does not belong to any other knowledge whatever." Cf. 1. Cor. ii. 11.

the most human interpretation of all the tremendous movements that we observe around us.

Of course, I know that, as a last resort, this "will" in us may be point-blank denied. But so may anything else (however certain) be denied with a little hardihood and a certain taste for paradox. It is often said, for instance, that the will may be resolved into motives; when, in fact, it is merely stimulated by motives. Or, again, its history may be investigated, and the cerebrum may be watched as it grew—from the amphioxus onwards. Very likely, and very interesting, too. But, however grown, and whatever made of, the Will is now positively there. It is a primary fact of human consciousness—like a colour or a sound. No man can either prove a colour or disprove it. He can only assert it, and call attention to it. And if his comrade be blind, he may not believe in its existence. If he be disputatious, and given to wrangle about words, he may say, "I have with a lens investigated your plate of green sand: it is not green, it is blue grains and yellow grains mixed; there is no such thing, therefore, as green." What can you do? You know it is green, and walk away. Controversy in such a case is useless.

Lastly, there is yet one more theory of the origin of all things, which must be mentioned; because it is a favourite theory with some men heartily devoted to science, who embrace it,—I think in a spirit of opposition to the Christian doctrine of Creation,—from not seeing to what irrational conclusions it ultimately leads. The theory I refer to is that of "chance," as the ultimate principle which accounts for all the present phenomena of the universe. It is not, however, necessary to spend much time in discussing this extraordinarily irrational supposition. There are facts, no doubt, which seem at first to look that way; as, for instance, the haphazard waste of seeds and of fishes' ova, the chance way in which strata and sea-beaches seem piled up, the capricious changes in the weather, and so forth. And hence some people, both in ancient and modern times, have been led to see in the cosmos itself only "a fortuitous concourse of atoms;" and have said, "Give me infinite past time,—and, after an infinite number of failures, the present complex harmony of Nature may conceivably have been attained."[1]

To this it may be replied, Can any stretch of human imagination conceive a box of letters thrown repeatedly on the floor, till at last they shall arrange themselves into a play of Shakspeare or the *Iliad* of Homer? Or again, How can infinite time be granted when both geology

[1] Büchner, *Der Gottesbegriff*, p. 29.

and astronomy loudly protest that, a comparatively short time ago, this earth was a mass of molten lava, on which no life could possibly exist? Both these objections, I think, hold good. But there is another, which is at least equally fatal. It is this: That the crude and childish conception of "chance" explains nothing and helps no one. It is a mere word, and is devoid of any sense or meaning. It carries our thoughts out, beyond the sphere of the human and the intelligible, into the inexplicable and irrational. It brings nothing home to us, awakens no intuition, arms us with no new powers of comprehension. It cannot pretend to excuse itself as a suggestion of as yet undiscovered "law;" for then it would be "chance" no longer. Law and chance are two mutually exclusive ideas. And if the noble, human, and fruitful conception of universal law in Nature is now, at last, to give way, and the un-human, chaotic notion of "a reign of haphazard" is to take its place, we shall have to bid a long and sorrowful adieu to science. For something reigns, it appears, in the universe which is utterly capricious, unreasonable, incalculable, incommensurate with the faculties of the human mind. All positive knowledge, therefore, and all forecast of the future become utterly impossible. No one can tell what may happen to-morrow, or lay down any fixed rules for his thoughts. The age of science, in short, has come to an end; and the infancy of mankind has returned, when Nature seemed without continuity or coherence, and we lived in an atmosphere of miracle and wonder, not knowing at any time what might happen next.

Such a theory of the origin of things is, surely, puerile. And as the notion of Fate is almost equally ridiculous, answering every question by the fatuous reply, "It is because it is;" while in the rational and suggestive theory of evolution there is nothing which conflicts with Christian teaching; we seem brought back at last, with thankful satisfaction, to that only hypothesis which is (so to speak) synchronous and in tune with the human intellect, majestic and beautiful to the human imagination, and full of animating confidence for the human heart, viz., the hypothesis of a Divine Creation, the doctrine that "in the beginning GOD created the heavens and the earth."

LECTURE IV.

MIRACLE.

ACTS xv. 19 : "Wherefore my sentence is, that we trouble not them which, from among the Gentiles, are turned to God."

LECT. IV.

WE reach to-day a subject from which—I am afraid—all scientific men turn away with an instinctive feeling of uneasiness and repugnance. It is the subject of *Miracles*. They think that the Church is hopelessly at variance with them on this question: and perhaps they suspect that she does not care to look it fairly and candidly in the face. I shall endeavour to show that this suspicion is not well-founded. And, on the other hand, I hope to be able to point out why, and how far, a greater liberty should nowadays be conceded by the Church to men of education in dealing with this question. For of this I am quite sure, that if a fuller liberty be not (in some way) accorded than it has been the custom to accord in times gone by, the tension between science and religion will ere long become so severe that the calamity will be imminent which Romanism, with its unyielding policy, has brought upon so many countries of the Continent; and our people, too, will be severed into hostile camps of superstition on one side and unbelief on the other. Hitherto England has had the good fortune, or the wisdom, to avoid this great calamity; and, owing to her faithful acceptance of the Reformation in the sixteenth century, she now possesses the "catholic" or traditional system of the Church in a reasonable and elastic form.

But English Christianity is in these days summoned to higher efforts still. And as our country has long ago, in politics, learnt and taught the lesson of patience, tolerance, and constant self-adaptation to the emerging changes of the world, so, in religion, it is now open to her to show *how a little timely deference and breadth of view may retain modern culture and science in allegiance to Christ*, and may preserve for men of thought and leisure the priceless blessing of unbroken religious communion with their less educated countrymen. The crucial problem, the turning-point on which the direction of the whole future depends, is the question of MIRACLE. Here stands the most solid of all modern "obstacles to Christian belief:" here gather, as to a focus, almost all the lines both of scientific and of literary objection.[1] For no educated European doubts any longer that law reigns supreme in Nature; and no well-read man or woman is ignorant that Miracle enters, as an essential ingredient, into every early history of every race and of almost every religion. At the same time, no one desires to find in God any traces of arbitrary or impulsive action. On the contrary, steadfastness and continuity are to us the "signs" of a Divine hand, and we should fail to recognise an arbitrary god as God at all. Hence "Miracle" has become to many of our generation a burden to be borne, an obstacle to be got over; it is, to them, no longer a help, but a hindrance. And yet (as has been well said) "there never was a time when the fundamental doctrines of Christianity could be more boldly proclaimed, or when they could better secure the respect and arrest the interest of science."[2] It seems, then, that the time is ripe for reviewing the whole question of Miracles, for a better ordering of the approaches to that

---

[1] "The miracles, which are so closely interwoven with the sacred story, look strange and out of place in a world where law is universal and invariable."—(Beard, *Hibbert Lecture*, 1883, p. 404.) "It would be hopeless to define the evidence which could establish the reality of the alleged occurrences."—(*Supernatural Religion*, iii. 403.)

[2] Drummond, *Natural Law in the Spiritual World*, 7th edition, p. 162.

obstacle, and for skilfully rearranging the defences of Christianity on that side.[1] It were not well if a slothful or obstinate retention of the ancient outworks—now turned—should cause the citadel to fall. Rather we need diligence (as St. Anselm says) to "work hard, when once we have attained a firm faith, to bring it into accord with reason;"[2] since (as St. Bernard still more forcibly puts it), "a faith, which admits of combination with any known error, is no Catholic Faith at all, but only a mistaken credulity."[3]

(1.) Now this last quotation from one of the most revered Fathers of the Church, singularly enough, places us precisely at the point of view which is occupied by M. Renan, and by all the most advanced thinkers of the present time. They say, We do not at all deny the *possibility* of Miracles: we are too painfully conscious of human limitation and infirmity to do that.[4] What we

---

[1] "Miracles have retired into the background as arguments for Christianity."—(Lias, *Are the Scripture Miracles Credible?* p. 255.) "To us, who for nineteen centuries have been children of that kingdom, such evidence is needless."—(Archd. Farrar, *Life of Christ*, 1874, i. p. xvi.) So too Augustine, *Confessions*, bk. xiii. § 29.

[2] *Cur Deus Homo*, i. 2.   [3] *Sermon* iv.

[4] "Ce n'est point par un raisonnement *à priori* que nous repoussons le miracle; c'est par un raisonnement critique ou historique. Plus on s'éloigne, plus la preuve d'un fait surnaturel devient difficile. Pour bien comprendre cela, il faut avoir

demand is that each case of supposed "Miracle" shall be subject to fair historical inquiry; so that if found to be a "*mythus*" it shall be truthfully acknowledged to be such; if found to be a "*legend*" it shall be guarded faithfully from being handled as if it were entirely without alloy; while if found on thorough historical investigation to be "*history*," then it shall be accepted exactly as it stands, and shall be treated—just as in physical science some new and surprising fact is treated—as a summons to set our little structure of preconceptions into better order, and to reflect that "there are more things in heaven and earth than were dreamed of perhaps in our philosophy."

Now this position of St. Bernard, of M. Renan, of Professor Huxley, of Professor Tyndall, Professor Helmholtz,[1] and of a host of scientific men in every land, is precisely the position also of English Christianity. With us, too, (so-called) edification is not the main thing; truth is the main thing. A God of truth, we are sure, cannot be served by a lie. Rather—as St. Augustine [2]

---

l'habitude de la critique des textes et de la méthode historique."
—(Renan, *Souvenirs*, 9th edition, p. 238.) "That miracles are impossible, being a wholly groundless assumption, the question of their actual occurrence becomes one of purely historical evidence."—(Shairp, *Culture and Religion*, 5th edition, p. 117.)

[1] *Ap.* Naville, *La Physique moderne*, p. 45.
[2] Augustine, *De Doctr. Christ.* lib. ii § 18.

so nobly puts it—we regard all truth, wherever found, as the royal metal (so to speak); and, in whatever remote place or whatever comminuted condition we light upon any shining morsel of real truth, that we claim at once as belonging to our Lord and King, and through Him to His Church. To this doctrine every intelligent Churchman will, without hesitation, at once accede. And therefore, whatever patience or caution he may think fit to display, he really desires with all his heart and soul *historical* veracity, as well as every other kind of veracity; and is as determined as any student of Nature can possibly be to stand or fall only by what is TRUE.

And if this be the case, surely one of the most imposing obstacles to churchmanship at once falls away and disappears. For it is (I think) the supposed engagement to maintain, at all hazards, certain things known to be untrue,[1] which

---

[1] Those who are surprised by statements and arguments which look this way should, however, remark the admissions which often accompany them; *e.g.*, "We are bound to tell mankind that these miracles were the method by which He manifested His character. He worked miracles. If you do not believe this, we have nothing more to say."—(Lias, *Are the Scripture Miracles Credible?* p. 255.) And yet some line must be drawn: for "we are bound to admit that the stoppage of the rotation of the earth is an unusual event. . . . There seems a high probability that, at a later period, some scribe added the quotation from another ancient history, the Book of Jasher."—(*Ibid.*

LECT. IV.

repels from the Church so many votaries of truth. But this supposition is an absolutely groundless one. On the contrary, whoever accepts the baptism of Jesus Christ, and lays the hand of loyalty in His hand, becomes from that hour a liegeman of *"the Truth;"* he hears the welcome reminder, "He that is of the Truth heareth my voice;" and (while avoiding fretful haste and reckless breach of charity) he is, and always must be, ready to weave in, at all cost, to the tissue of Christian thought whatever time shall verify as true, and to eliminate, as alien and foreign matter, whatever may ultimately show itself as untrue. For no infallibility with us stops the way. Even the general councils of the Church we allow may err, and have erred, in things pertaining to God. And therefore, surely, all such liberty of thought and speech as any reasonable and calm and charitable man ought to desire is already *ipso facto*, as a Christian, his. No one can rob him of that right. And every help he can himself bring to the elimination of falsehood from Christian

p. 228.) And, with regard to the sun-dial of Ahaz, "the possibility of later interpolations is becoming more and more clearly acknowledged."—(*Ibid.* p. 231.) Again, "Does the inspiration of the Bible necessarily imply the correctness of every statement contained in it? I think that it does."—(Bishop Perry, *Science and the Bible*, 1869, p. 75.) But still, "tradition does not show the deluge to have extended over the whole earth; which seems to have been disproved by geology."—(*Ibid.* p. 71.)

doctrine is welcome, if only offered in the spirit of courteous patience and charity for those who have been long used to other ways of thinking. If then want of liberty in dealing with the question of Miracles be alleged as an obstacle to Christian belief, the answer is plain and decisive: No such want of liberty exists. Truth alone is what we Christians, like all other men, are interested in. Truth alone is what we, as Christians, are bound earnestly to seek and faithfully to hold fast.[1] And the Church of Jesus Christ has nothing whatever to do with anything which is not true.

(2.) But we must now go further than this, and must explain the Christian position with regard to Miracles more clearly. For there exists a second obstacle to belief in the shape of a deeply-rooted misapprehension as to what the Church really means by a "Miracle." It is commonly alleged that by her acceptance of Miracle she derogates in some way from the majestic and now firmly-established conception of permanent law in Nature; because it is supposd that *miraculous* and *capricious* action are identical. No better

---

[1] "O veritas, veritas! Quam intimè, etiam tum [æt. 18] medullæ animi mei suspirabant tibi!"—(Augustine, *Confessions*, lib. iii. § 10.) "Bishop Butler said, 'I mean to make truth the business of my life.'"—(*The Century*, September, 1884.)

exponent of this view could be found than Hartmann, in the following remarkable passage: "So long as Miracle is not regarded as contradicting Nature, there is, in reality, no reasonable ground for protesting against it—except the character of *caprice*, which it presents."[1] But miracle is certainly not regarded nowadays as "contradicting" Nature. It is simply regarded—whenever it can be proved to have occurred at all, which is purely a matter for history to determine—as a point of intersection between some vast outer circle of God's ways and the small inner circle to which we ourselves are better accustomed.[2] It is as though a meteor or a comet of vast orbit abruptly came and went within our smaller terrestrial orbit. The Miracle then, of course, consists solely in the intersection being of set purpose, harmonised and arranged to act as a "sign" and a moral force upon certain observers.

Now against such a Miracle even John Stuart Mill acknowledges that no valid objection can be raised, short of a doubt or denial of God altogether. For he says, "There are few things of which we have more frequent experience than

---

[1] *Darwinisme*, p. 160.

[2] "The mediæval belief in miracles, and the modern belief in law, cannot be held by the same mind."—(Dr. Flint, *On Theism*, 1877, p. 13.)

of physical facts which our knowledge does not
enable us to account for, because they depend on
'laws' which observation, aided by science, has
not yet brought to light; and it is always possible
that the wonder-worker may have acquired (consciously or unconsciously) the power of calling
these into action. . . . We cannot, then, conclude
absolutely that the miraculous theory ought to be
at once rejected. . . . Once admit a God, and the
production of an effect by His direct volition
must be reckoned with as a serious possibility."[1]
Yes, this is surely true; and Mr. Mill has here
touched, as with a needle's point, the narrow and
(it may be hoped) vanishing line which separates
the believer from the non-believer in Miracles.
Once admit a God, and you admit "volition" in
Nature.

Does, then, the abrupt revelation of "new law"
involve, of necessity, the notion of "caprice?"
To this it may be replied: First, that science
itself has frequently to admit the existence of
new—yet certainly not capricious—laws. For instance, it was always confidently believed that
all substances contract by cold, till at last it was
discovered that water and bismuth expand by
cold.[2] Again, the circulation of the blood was, till

---

[1] J. S. Mill, *Essays on Religion*, p. 230.
[2] Tyndall, *Heat*, p. 86.

1824, supposed to follow an invariable direction, but in that year a new law of *alternation* came to light in a certain Ascidian.[1] In 1861, M. Comte's unfortunate prediction that no one would ever find out the chemical composition of the solar bodies, was stultified by the sudden apparition of a new law of incandescent gases. And not long ago, after ages of unalleviated pain, a new law of anæsthetics suddenly broke upon mankind. It is clear we are absolutely surrounded and enveloped by an unseen *world* of latent, undiscovered, unsuspected "laws." It may be, therefore, that "Miracle" is but the well-timed (not capricious) apparition of some new law,[2] some unsuspected reason, some undiscovered faculty. And if so, after producing its purposed moral and spiritual effect, the "wonder" may be capable afterwards (if God will) of gradual resolution into terms of our ordinary intelligence.

Secondly: if some element of "caprice," appear to exist in the *harmonising* of times and concurrences, which it seems as if God had kept in His own power,—still this "harmonising and timing" process is going on in the realm of

---

[1] Huxley, *Lay Sermons*, p. 95.
[2] "Omnia portenta contra Naturam dicimus esse. Sed non sunt. . . . Portentum fit, non contra naturam, sed contra quam [eam quæ] est nota natura."—(Augustine, *Civ. Dei*, xxi. 8.)

nature, at every moment and in every direction, around us. Bees go forth in the morning, and all day long they visit only one species of flower,[1] in order that pollen may be carried where alone it will succeed. The eye is prepared in secret, where no light has access; and when sunshine at last reaches it, it sees. And so, no doubt, in *human* history, too, every harmonising process proceeds by law and by reason; for, as Mr. Mill truly says, "We cannot but suppose the Deity, in every one of His acts, to be guided by motives."[2] Yes, to think otherwise would be treason against God. What! are we to exaggerate our fancies so far, and accumulate to such an intolerable height all the old world's pictorial and childish conceptions of the Deity—which is arming, at this very hour, the bloody hand of Islam once more—as to make God an awful Eastern Despot, an arbitrary Sesostris or a Nebuchadnezzar, whose nod is death, and whose whims and passions, as they chase each other across his mind, decide the destinies of a universe? Away with so blasphemous a thought! Un-reason has no place whatever in the Christian conception of God. Rather He is "the Amen," the faithful and steadfast and true, in Whom is "no variableness,

---

[1] Lubbock, *Flowers in Relation to Insects,* 1882, p. 26.
[2] *Essays,* p. 228.

neither shadow of turning." St. Paul, in his Second Epistle to the Corinthians,[1] bases an elaborate argument on this very axiom of the Gospel. And just as, in the noblest and best and most regal of men, *the most firm and stable and continuous and unvacillating purpose* displays itself, so (surely) the Christian is bound to think it is with God. Caprice, then, is absolutely excluded. God would not be God if He were not the supreme reason and the source of steadfast transcendent order. And, if any Miracle should ever proceed from His hand, we may (and we must) conceive that it, too, is but the fragmentary arc of some vast curve, whose "law" may not be known to us, but is certainly known to Him.[2]

Thus any "obstacle to belief" which may have arisen from the notion that Miracle contravenes the sublime idea of universal and inviolable law, turns out to be a purely imaginary obstacle. Let history only do its part, and positively assure us of the actual occurrence of any miraculous event, and we are at once at home again in a wider sweep of "law" than we had moved in

---

[1] 2 *Cor.* i. 20.
[2] "Les sciences naturelles ont dû souvent reconnaître des faits en apparence incroyables et contraires à toutes les lois généralement acceptées."—(Oscar Schmidt, *Phil. de l'Inconscient*, French translation, p. 91.)

before. Our horizon is enlarged—that is all. And, as men of sense and modesty, we begin at once to conform our ways of thinking to the new environment amid which we find ourselves, and to readjust our too narrow theories to the newly-ascertained facts.

(3.) And this brings us to another thought, the pursuit of which may help to confirm our liberty in dealing with this baffling subject of Miracle. It is certain that Miracles, if they really happened, and if they came from God, must have been employed by Him for some definite *purpose*. They were not "portents," scattered at random about the universe, confounding the wise and astonishing the simple. Rather they were "signs," with a moral and religious end in view.[1] They were helps towards the construction of some great system of belief, a schooling to train us amid childish things for a higher maturity, a scaffolding to assist—while it veiled for a time—the elevation of some permanent edifice of thought, in relation to which the scaffolding was a mere temporary expedient. When, therefore, the build-

---

[1] "The significance of the miracle is its manifestation of a divine power. But we have, in present reality, that transcendent power which Christ's truth and grace are at this moment exercising over the world."—(Bp. Barry, *Boyle Lectures*, 1880, p. 206.) "History, with us, takes the [evidential] place of prophecy."—(*Ibid.* p. 204.)

ing was completed, the scaffolding surely might be dispensed with. Rather, it must of necessity be dispensed with; else it will begin to hinder where it formerly helped.

Take, for instance, the two great series of Miracles which are alleged to have accompanied and assisted the building up of the Jewish and then of the Christian dispensation. What was the purpose—what was, at any rate, the actual effect—of each of those series of wonders, as they are related upon the pages of the Bible? It was, in the first case, the building up of a solid and afterwards never-questioned monotheism. And that point once absolutely secured, the scaffolding ceased to be of much use or even of much interest. And so, not only the Old Testament Miracles, but at last (as we are happily reminded by St. James in the text) the entire elaborate mechanism of the Mosaic institutions — divine though they were, and admirably adapted to their temporary purpose—became actually obsolete and "ready to vanish away."[1] Its work was done. And when it was attempted by some, whose loyalty to the past was greater than their foresight of the future, to maintain the Mosaic Law unchanged, it became an obstacle to true belief. The letter began to confine and strangle the spirit. The

---

[1] *Hebrews* viii. 13.

real made war against the ideal. And the whole lifetime of the greatest and most energetic of the Apostles, subsequent to his conversion, was expended in securing for the Gentile world a complete emancipation from the school-methods which Israel had gone through. In other words, *it was not the method, but the result, which was prized by God and was valuable to man.* " Let not them be troubled," therefore, with Jewish rites and Levitical ceremonies, " which from among the Gentiles are turned to God."

And the same process had to be repeated during the long twilight of the Dark Ages and the infancy of the modern European nations. The science of that day was quite incompetent to teach mankind the unity of all things. It preferred to break up Nature into separate kingdoms. Its fancy peopled the earth with magical and irrational agents. And Nature threatened to become, under its teaching, an assemblage of independent forces and independent principles.[1] Indeed, this failure of science to teach mankind the oneness of the Cosmos reached almost down to our own time; and (as Mr. Mill confesses) only "a few generations

---

[1] For instance, "There existed all through the Middle Ages, and even as late as the seventeenth century, the sect of the Cabalists. They believed in the existence of 'spirits of nature,' embodiments or representatives of the four elements."—(Lecky, *History of Rationalism*, 2nd edition, i. 46.)

ago the dependence of phenomena on universal laws was unrecognised by mankind: and even by the instructed could not be regarded as a scientifically established truth."[1] But during all that weary time, the Church had always persistently taught it, in her doctrine of the One God; and religion had maintained that healthful atmosphere of Monotheism,[2] amid which alone the grand truth of Nature's unity could gradually and tentatively be reached by science. But how, amid the then complexity and childishness of physics, was the Church able to keep in mind this Divine unity of all things? It was, I think, mainly through the conception of *Miracle;* which seemed to men to reveal, in glimpses and in patches, the underlying Divine government—in other words, the unity of all things—and so heralded the clear scientific acknowledgment of it, as patches of open water herald the emancipation of the Arctic spring.

And precisely the same thing may be said with regard to the second great series of Miracles, which assisted in building up the early stages of the Christian dispensation. As the popular belief in

---

[1] *Essays*, p. 222.

[2] "Men's creed is perpetually changing under the influence of civilization. In the Middle Ages the measure of probability was essentially theological. Men seemed to breathe an atmosphere that was entirely unsecular."—(Lecky, *Rationalism*, i. 88.)

the Old Testament Miracles engendered among the Jews a monotheistic conception of the world, which (after the Captivity) nothing was able to destroy; and as the mediæval Miracles taught new barbaric Europe the same conception, which (since the Reformation) nothing has been able to undermine; so the New Testament Miracles engendered a firm belief in Christ, and a conception of Him as "the image" or incarnation of God's thought concerning man,[1] whereby that ineffable thought was rendered visible, tangible, intelligible. There is no doubt that this remarkable effect has really been produced. For the modern world is positively permeated with the conviction of the sublime mission of Jesus Christ, and is penetrated to the heart by the touching beauty of His character. Those who have brought themselves to deny every one of His Miracles yet confess, with Dr. Strauss, that " Jesus appears as a thoroughly lovely character, needing only to be developed from within, and never needing anything like a conversion or a beginning afresh,"[2]—in short, with nothing to repent of, sinless. And those who most despair

LECT. IV.

---

[1] Ἐγέννησεν ὁ Πατὴρ τὸν Υἱὸν . . . λόγον, οὐ προφορικὸν ἀλλ' ἐνυπόστατον καὶ ζῶντα, οὐ χείλεσι λαληθέντα ἀλλ' ἐκ Πατρὸς ἀϊδίως καὶ ἀνεκφράστως. Λόγος νοῶν τοῦ Πατρὸς τὸ βούλημα. . . . Λόγος λαλῶν καὶ λέγων "Ἃ ἑώρακα παρὰ τῷ Πατρί μου, ταῦτα λαλῶ.—(Cyril of Jerus., *Lectures*, xi.)   [2] *Leben Jesu*, p. 208.

of acquiring any true knowledge about religious matters, say, "People no longer ask for Miracles or for the authority assigned to Miracles. The plain demand is, Tell us of Christ! Tell us all you know, or deem you know, about Christ! Assist us with your learning, that we may understand and correctly appreciate what is written concerning Him. The more these demands are acceded to, the more resplendent do the work and mission of Christ appear."[1]

Thus, by whatever means it has been produced, it is certain that a profound appreciation of Jesus Christ has come to be almost universally attained amongst civilised mankind. We have not seen Christ. A hundred obscurities and difficulties and perplexities beset His wonderful biography. They were meant, perhaps, to loosen our attachment to the mere "letter" of the gospel. Nevertheless His "spirit," has seized us. His ideal remains photographed upon our minds, though much of that which helped to fix it there may perchance have been washed away. And as a young man is haunted, and his character is often quite transfigured, by the ever-present image of one he loves, so the world to whom Jesus has been preached is haunted, and is being transformed by His ideal. The Miracles, therefore,

---

[1] Bithell, *Creed of a Modern Agnostic*, p. 126.

which at first propped up and protected this faith, and which (as all allow) have long ago ceased, may perhaps be meant to become henceforth of historical, rather than religious, interest. And a race of mankind, which has permanently acquired this conception, may perhaps justly claim that it should not henceforth be "troubled" overmuch by things that were once a help, but are now a difficulty. It may be permitted to draw near to Christ by avenues that are to it more appropriate and easy. And it may be allowed to fall back upon our Lord's "last benediction of the Gospel and special endowment of the later Church,"[1] viz., "Blessed are they that have not seen [with outward miraculous evidences], and yet have believed."

We may even illustrate this position by observing what is going on under our very eyes, in relation to belief in the Holy Spirit and His personal agency among men. We see, at the present day, how many men are helped to a thorough grasp of this doctrine—in some respects the greatest and most influential doctrine of our time—by a conviction of His almost sensible presence in their crowded assemblies, and by a belief in something as near "miraculous" agency[2]

---

[1] Westcott, *Gospel of the Resurrection*, p. 102.
[2] Cf. Drummond, *Natural Law*, p. 94.

as the uncongenial atmosphere of our day will allow. But when once they have reached and grasped the doctrine, have assimilated it, and find themselves actually growing stronger and riper every day by His mysterious presence within them, they do not suffer themselves (I think) to be seriously perplexed and shaken by the remembrance of their past excitement and enthusiasm, and of the marvels by which they were formerly helped. *They have got the reality; they have built the house.* The "sign," therefore, and the scaffolding have become things of the past; and if "difficulties" arise about them, they are difficulties that need no longer perplex.

But if thus in all departments of Christian doctrine—relating to the Father, the Son, and the Holy Spirit—it be true that Miracle has wholly or partially done its work, has retired into the background, and has ceased to be an assistance to belief, may we not gather all these facts together into a general statement, and say that the interest and importance of Miracles, as a whole, has past (or is passing) away; and that a feverish, anxious quest about them is as little required of Christians in the nineteenth century, as a nervous scrupulosity about the Mosaic Law was required in the first century? Why should it be required? When once the goal has been attained, why should all the way we came be so anxiously scanned afresh? Why should all the past stepping-stones be revisited and carefully scrutinised; the weak and perilous foot-bridges be suspiciously tested, and gone over again; and the things that are *before* be forgotten, that we may press back to those things that are *behind?* Do you say, "We cannot be sure that we have arrived, unless we thus go over the whole journey again?" But, surely, a man who looks round and finds himself in London, does not vex his soul about the state of the rails or the structure of the engine that has brought him there. And so, to a man who has really grasped and assimilated the magnificent idea of Monotheism, what does it greatly matter whether the story of Samson be a mythus or not; whether Balaam's history be mingled with legend or not; whether Joshua's miracle be taken from the book of Jasher, or not? whether Jonah's prophecy be poetry or prose? These things have now taken, for him, their true position and their real value. *They are historical and literary questions of the utmost interest. They are religious questions no longer.*

And in the same way, if a man have once realised the unique majesty and beauty of CHRIST's character, and his heart have fallen in love (so to speak) with that sublime Personality—what are to such a man the petty baffling questions about the New Testament Miracles? Rather would he smile, when urged to deny Christ on their account, and would say (with aged Polycarp): "So many years have I known and served him; how *can* I now forsake my Saviour and my King?" Or he would exclaim, with St. Paul: "Yea, though [in times gone by] I may have known Christ after the flesh, henceforth know I Him [thus] no more."

We can, therefore, and if we can we ought, to gather calmness, cheerfulness, and courage from the commanding positions which—both in Science and Religion—we have now attained; so that breathing this serener air, we may address ourselves with confidence to the great historical and physical studies which lie before us, and by means of which the true is to be sifted from the false. And then perhaps, at last, faith and patience may receive an unexpected reward. A larger and freer view of the vast possibilities, which the universe has in store, may emancipate our minds from too much narrowness in denial. And, candidly weighing the force of evidence, we may at length be able to say, "It is not by reasoning *à priori*, nor yet by a blind submission to authority, that we have come to believe in certain Miracles of the Gospel; but by arguments drawn from criticism and history."

For, in all human things (as the saying is), "well begun is half done." In innumerable cases, to begin at the right end is the whole secret of ultimate success. And in these subtle religious questions (above all) to begin building at the bottom rather than the top—to begin, *e.g.*, with the *human nature* of Christ[1] and advance from that as high as you can, to begin with the mere *symbolism* of the Sacraments and rise from that to higher thoughts about them, to begin with the plain *historical facts* and political environment of Christ's life, and to mount from them to the higher and more difficult conceptions of His nature and His mission to mankind—*that* is true policy. That sets a man on his way to a firm and solid belief; that removes a hundred obstacles and stumbling-blocks, and mountain-ranges of difficulty out of his way, by simply starting him *along* them (as it were) instead of athwart them. That, in short, is the Apostles' system; who always began, in heathen countries, by preaching in Jewish synagogues and to people somewhat "prepared for the Lord." That is Christ's own method; Who always began with easy things and went on to harder things, and

---

[1] "If any do not include the supernatural character of Christianity in their definition of it, the support of miracles is not wanted; because the moral truths are their own evidence."—(Mozley, *On Miracles*, 1st edition, p. 22.)

was contented to see "first the blade, then the ear, then the full corn in the ear."

Approached in this way—left to the last, instead of being presented, in all its deterring perplexity to the modern man, at the threshold of the inquiry after Christ—Miracle ceases to be an obstacle to Christian belief. The gentle and tolerant maxim of the Saviour comes into play, "He that is able to receive it, let him receive it." There will always be an abundance of people fully able to receive it. Let not him that receiveth judge him that receiveth not: for he may be on his way to a full reception. To be a liegeman of Christ is to be a Christian—unless the Apostles who left all and followed Him, without even understanding as yet His Jewish Messiahship, were not "Christians." The question which is put by Christ to every man is like the question of Jehu in the Old Testament, "Is thy heart right, as my heart is with thy heart? If it be, give me thine hand." It were absurd to suppose that a harassing course of historical criticism must come first; it were maddening to be assured that salvation hung suspended on an exhaustive metaphysical inquiry into the nature and evidential force of Miracle. It hangs suspended on something better—on a decision of the heart, rather than of the intellect. And just as millions are devoted Christians, whose intellects are clouded with the grossest superstitions, so may thousands be devoted Christians and be at inward peace with God, whose intellects are beset with subtle doubts and are daily engaged with historical and other problems, for whose solution a lifetime is insufficient.

Let a man once cast off, with a sense of its puerile grotesqueness, the notion of a universe given over to Chance—let a man, by an act of his will, repudiate the chilling and irrational conception of a universe ruled by dead Fate—and let him believe with all his heart in a living God and a super-human (not infra-human) conscious Will at the world's helm: such an one is not far from the kingdom of heaven. He has entered upon the avenue which leads, if diligently pursued to the end, to a moral knowledge of the invisible God. He is on his way to recognize in Christ an incomparable *teacher* about God, One Who "spake as never man spake." Learning and appreciating those lessons, he will come to feel that never, on the world's stage, has any such *presentment* of a divinely-human character as Christ's been ever exhibited to God and to man. And bowing heart and conscience in allegiance to this great Master, he will reach at last a peaceful rest beneath Christ's gentle *reign*. And acknowledging thus, by a slow and natural growth of conviction, Christ to be his "prophet, priest, and king," such a man ought to find among the Christian clergy helpers, friends, and guides. He ought to meet with welcome from skilful ministers of the New Testament, who "make straight paths lest that which is lame be turned out of the way,"[1] and who hold with calm assurance that "the reliance of the clergy must be in liberty: that their power does not lie in traditions treasured up from the past, but in their sympathy with the aspirations of the future: and that religious discussion and inquiry conduct to progress, which after all is but the pursuit of light."[2]

[1] *Hebrews* xii. 13.
[2] Esquiros, *Religious Life in England*, sub fin.

LECTURE V.

THE FALL OF MAN.

GEN. iii. 7 : "And the eyes of them both were opened; and they knew that they were naked."

WHERE will you find, within the whole field of human literature, a sentence so full of profound ethical truth as this? Where will you light upon fifteen words that so simply, and yet so accurately, depict a universal fact of moral consciousness; that refer us with such unerring point and certainty to the discovery which (I fear) we have each one made long ago for ourselves — viz., that, alone among all living creatures upon the earth, we have cause to feel "shame"? Yes: explain it how you will, attenuate it by pointing out some indistinct traces of a similar feeling in one or two of the very highest domesticated animals, still the indisputable fact remains—that "shame" is a universal

LECT. V.

characteristic of the human species; and that a "shameless man" is an abnormal being for whom all his fellow-creatures blush.

Whence, then, arises this singular proclivity to shame? What have we all done, that this uneasy suspicion should haunt us that all is not as it should be? It is quite useless to divert attention from the fact; or to conceal it from observation behind gaiety of demeanour or an air of absorption in the world's pursuits. The truth always emerges, in spite of our best efforts to conceal it, that "conscience doth make cowards of us all." From the deepest depths of the past, a proud, conquering Pharaoh speaks to us on the embankment-obelisk; and even he talks of seeking peace to his conscience.[1] A pure, high-minded philosopher, like Marcus Aurelius, feels impelled to say, "O my soul, when wilt thou be such as to need pardon no longer from the gods and from men?"[2] A rapt and devoted Christian saint, like Augustine, is forced to cry out, "What can bring us back to hope, except God's mercy?"[3]

[1] "Thothmes III. occupied the throne of Egypt about 1450 B.C. This is one of the few dates that can be authenticated." ... On the fourth side of the obelisk, the highest authorities read, that Thothmes hoped for repose to his mind from the fact that he made due offerings to the gods. (King, *Cleopatra's Needle*, pp. 61, 94.)

[2] *Private Thoughts*, Book x., § 1.

[3] *Confessions*, Book x., § 58.

And from the page of the modern German unbeliever rises the same sad confession: "In the self-assertion of the flesh against the spirit I recognise sin: and since man is by nature subject to this tyranny of the flesh, it follows that he is by nature sinful: and, the sinful nature propagating itself, there arises an *original* sinfulness."[1] Thus from every quarter of the human horizon alike there reaches our ear the same strange note of discord and dissatisfaction, the same confession of moral incapacity and failure, the same unrest and sense of shame.

And then reflect that this note is heard from no other creature whatever, besides man, on all this broad earth. The animals around us, throughout their tribes, are naked and are not ashamed. There is no sense of sin apparent among them, although their actions are often such as—for cruelty, selfishness, greed, impurity —should awaken the keenest sense of shame. But they are evidently not capable of such a feeling. Man alone is capable of it; because (as Dr. Büchner tells us) "it is only in man that the world becomes conscious to such a degree, that it rises out of its previous dream-like natural existence. Struggle, therefore, now rages on the

---

[1] Frauenstädt, *Religion der Natur*, p. 176.

LECT. V.

domain of morals as violently as it formerly did on the physical field."[1]

It becomes, then, at this point, extremely interesting to inquire *at what precise moment, in every one's life, was this fatal venom of sin and shame introduced into his constitution?* We are all conscious of it now. Was it introduced yesterday, or at any other fixed point in our past lives? Nay: though I may have sinned yesterday, broken through the normal law of my being, clouded and confused the ideal of my life, that sin (I know too well) was preceded and generated by many other sins reaching back in sad procession to the furthest confines of my memory. And even the first sin that I can remember must have had a latent cause. It was, evidently, but the outcome of a strange *bias* to evil, which—in me, as in every other child of man—seems to be congenital. Thus it is impossible to put the finger on any certain hour or on any special event in any one's life, and to say, " Here first evil found an entrance into the soul. Before that fatal moment a spotless angel was among us, an evenly-balanced character, bearing no burden of hereditary bias, showing no discoloured trace of ancestral tendency to sin. It was purely white, a

[1] *Man in the Past, the Present, and the Future,* English translation, 1872, p. 150.

sheet of blank paper."[1] We all know that such a description would be absolutely false, and even "unscientific"; and that the Church's ancient ban against all such Pelagian heresy has since been abundantly confirmed by the best modern observation and the surest modern discoveries.[2]

But if so, if there is a strain of evil in every one of us, and no child of man, even by any favourable accident, ever escapes the taint, then one's thoughts are compelled to wander back beyond the individual life. The history of the *species* opens before us. And at some point in that history we have again to search where we may put our finger down and say, "Just there—in the reign of that king, on the day after that political crisis, at the precise moment when that tribe landed on a certain shore—sin began in the world." But, once more, of course we cannot do

[1] Dr. Moleschott appears to regard the human mind in this way. He says, "Pourvu qu'on accorde que la pensée n'est que la page sur laquelle viennent s'inscrire les faits, et qu'elle n'ait d'autre privilège que celui de les raconter, la glorie de la science est fondée."—(*Circulation de la Vie*, French translation, i. 22.)

[2] The Church's strong aversion to Pelagianism has been much discredited by her champions' injudicious language in the opposite direction. But "we may believe that the sin of the first man entailed on his posterity a condition of sinfulness, . . . while yet we may avoid language which would suggest a literal imputation of Adam's sin to each of his descendants; and admit that 'sin' can bear only a modified sense in regard to what is not personal."—(Dr. Bright, *Antipelagian Treatises of St. Augustine*, p. xiii.)

anything of the kind. The origin of sin again eludes us. And so conscious failure to do right, shameful divergence from known duty, seems to be primæval, and to haunt mankind like the shadow of some bright endowment. It is an "electric chain wherewith we are all darkly bound." And we must pass out beyond history itself, if we are to track this mischief to its source. In short, we are baffled; and we cannot do better than confess, with St. Augustine, St. Ambrose and St. Cyprian, that it flows down *ab origine*, and that it is, in a word, ORIGINAL SIN.

And yet, when we come to think of it, there must have been *some* "origo," *some* beginning of this evil. On all modern, as well as on all ancient, theories of the "descent of man," there certainly was a time when "shame," consciousness of failure, had not yet dawned upon him. Suppose, for instance, he came directly from the hand of God—surely, under that hypothesis, he was not placed upon this earth originally burdened with a horrible sense of guilt. Or suppose, as science nowadays prefers to put it, that man's frame was prepared for him by a long series of evolutions, and that "man is intimately allied by his origin to the whole chain of inferior organic forms,"[1]—still that makes no difference.

[1] Büchner, *Vie psychique des Bêtes*, French translation, p. 16.

On all suppositions alike, there must have been a certain moment when he made the grand transition and became, to all intents and purposes, a MAN; when he ceased to be either a dormant nonentity or a dreaming animal and awoke to self-consciousness. There must have been an hour when—just as plant-life had once upon a time *appeared*, or when animal-life had once upon a time *appeared*—so now spiritual, or reflexive self-conscious life, *appeared*.[1] And then upon this planet, for the first time, stood a being in whom had dawned a new and hitherto unheard-of power of self-determination, of self-judgment, and of self-reproach. It is true the circle within which these new powers of freedom could be exercised was, and is still, a very narrow one; and that he was, and is still, hemmed in by a compact hedge of inexorable outside laws, whose forces he may, to a certain small extent, combine and direct, but may neither break through nor contravene. But that limitation, again, makes no essential difference. Within his little circle, at any rate, this erect and vertebrated mammal awoke one day to a sense of freedom; awoke to find that the

[1] "This [Triassic] period is one of the most important turning-points in the organic history of the earth. The Palæolithic fern forests were then *replaced* by the pine forests ; and perhaps all remains of reptiles belong to the Trias onwards." —(Haeckel, *History of Creation*, English translation, ii. 221.)

supposed finality of the previous reign of brute life was no finality at all. Among the rich possibilities of creation there was latent yet another force, which was destined to change the whole face of the earth. And this force was the mental force of reflex, and therefore of accumulated, consciousness;[1] the power of self-reflection upon the laws of his being, of mental concurrence with them or of dissent from them; the duty of judging them and of judging himself; the choice of happy, willing self-surrender, or of shameful reproachful failure and moral downfall. Yes; the day had dawned, the hour had come. And a fall had, from that hour, become at any moment possible. But it had not yet actually occurred.

Would it, or would it not, occur? Might it be averted? Who could, at that fateful, that critical turning-point of all the world's future history, foretell the course of events? At any rate, no compromising deed had yet been done. And so—emerging (it may be) from the animal world of absolute and sinless unconsciousness—primæval

---

[2] "A partir de ce moment, les phénomènes conscients s'enchaînent l'un à l'autre : il y a de la mémoire. Cette coordination des impressions, en vue d'un but à attendre, devient un raisonnement. . . Enfin tout désir accompagné d'un raisonnement, d'une évaluation relative du mobile, devient une volition."—(Letourneau, *Physiologie des Passions*, second edition, 1878, p. 40.)

man stood there innocent, however capable now of falling. It must have been so. No other hypothesis is thinkable, no other sequence of events is conceivable. He was poised, then, for a moment ἐπὶ ξυροῦ ἀκμῆς,—as it were "on a razor's edge." How long could, or would, the equipoise be maintained?

Alas, too surely a fall would come. The ideal, mirrored in transient reality, of an innocent and yet no longer a merely animal being, was seen, only to be dashed after too short trial to the ground. And then man became conscious, not only that he possessed a new *power*, such as no dog or ape or ant or bee had ever possessed, but that—when once with powerful recoil the animal nature had reasserted itself—he possessed a new *feeling*. And so shame, self-reproach and conflict, began. Amid suffering and toil and bitter loss, this new acquisition of freedom must (like every other) through long ages be tested and tempered and trained to harmonious service. In short (to return to Biblical language), "the eyes of mankind were opened, and they *knew* that they were naked."

Now what is there in all this account of the origin of human guilt and self-reproach which should give any reasonable offence, or present any serious difficulty, to a candid and observant man? Is it the doctrine of "heredity,"—which is here presupposed? Is it the theory of selection by moral conflict, and of the ultimate survival of the fittest,—which here receives a consecration by theology? Surely these things are the corner-stones of all modern biological science. And it would rather seem as if Christianity had here again, as in so many other cases, by a kind of penetrating forecast, actually anticipated the course of modern thinking; and had long ago presented, in rude sketch and poetic adumbration, the very same truths as science was afterwards to make her own. What then are the "obstacles to Christian belief" which the Church's doctrine of the FALL OF MAN presents to a cultivated and refined intellect? With the utmost efforts to be scrupulously just, I can only imagine three objections:—

(1.) First of all, "*that this description of the fall of man contradicts (in some way) the reigning hypothesis of 'evolution'*; that a more reasonable and scientific account of the universal moral failure we see around us is to be found in the doctrine of unbroken 'bestial survivals' within us; that what we are called upon morally to do, therefore, is simply to 'let the ape and tiger die,'[1] to cultivate and raise to the highest efficiency

---

[1] Tennyson, *In Memoriam*, stanza cxvii.

and power the new faculties that have dawned within man, and so eventually to conquer a new platform (so to speak) of terrestrial life for our species. And then, perhaps, a new beginning shall be possible, and a new and higher race shall come into being." But to all this the reply, surely, is very easy. There is no contradiction whatever, there is a complete harmony, between this theory and the Christian representation of things. The Bible teaching, from the very fact of its being so pictorial and childlike, is most elastic and ready to welcome—like some well-devised political framework—every successive development and every healthful consolidation of structure that increasing knowledge can offer to its service. Indeed I am bold to say that the Church of God has, throughout its long life of eighteen hundred years, been incessantly occupied—just as the human body is, to which it offers so many striking analogies—in selecting from the stream of matter perpetually placed at its disposal that which it can build with, and in rejecting what is foreign and incompatible. Now all these hypotheses of evolution, of natural selection, of heredity, of survival, it *can* build with. The materials they offer are compatible with the life, and kindred with the doctrine of Christianity. They simply make more rational and intelligible, and expand into prose, what the Church has perhaps too vaguely and poetically taught. For as St. Clement of Alexandria puts it, "Science is the active clenching by reason of the passive acceptances of faith:"[1] to which St. Augustine generously adds, "Faith holds the door *open* for science to enter in."[2]

But Christian faith does even *more* for science than that. It very often—with its singularly wide and large poetry of anticipation—displays some half-finished but suggestive sketch, waiting (as it were) to be filled up in detail; and thereby it seems to invite science to yet further and more serious efforts.

Just so it is here. And science, with her conception of unbroken bestial-survivals, has not taken sufficient account of that momentary equipoise and subsequent downfall, which must have occurred when man first emerged from animal innocence and became really "man." Nor has it properly pictured out the full grandeur and truth of that strange evolution, *reflex consciousness* in man—in other words, human freewill—and of its consequences throughout a long and painful education. Nor yet has science sufficiently observed how many moral evils are now fully deve-

---

[1] Clement of Alexandria, *Strom.*, Book VII.
[2] Ap. Bishop Wordsworth, *on Genesis*, p. xxii.

loped in human nature, which are not "bestial" at all. Such are despair, pure diabolical destructiveness, utter scepticism, religious fanaticism, and many more. Thus there is an abundance of problems still waiting to be worked out, in every department both of scientific theory and of religious practice. Why should we not close our ranks and work fraternally together (as Christ would have us do) against all the protean forms of human misery, ignorance and sin?

(2.) But there is another and a far more trenchant reason why some men of science hold aloof from all co-operation with the Church; and why they especially detest her doctrine of the "fall of man." They say—though how they can say it passes one's comprehension—"*that man is innocent still: that he cannot have fallen, because he is not sinful now.* The failure which an unenlightened reason stigmatises as 'sin,' is not sin at all. It is hardly misfortune. The course of events, the stream of tendency, is responsible for its occurrence. And as to man, he has no free-will, and therefore no responsibility. He is, in fact, an animal still, an anthropoid mammal. He cannot help doing what he does; he cannot choose but follow whatever impulse, good or bad, is predominant for the moment. He is, in short, a machine. He is a marionette, pulled about by unseen wires of multifarious solicitation, and played, in some way, by the memories or by the newly-emergent instincts of the universal mother of all living things, Matter."

On this supposition, of course, all the theories of modern science about man's ascent from amid the brute world of unconscious and almost automatic dreaming, lose their sense and meaning. The story of his fall, too, from momentary equipoise becomes a nursery tale. And the animating hope of his recovery—and more than recovery—through conflict, toil, and pain, evaporates into haze and illusion. No evolution towards moral life and self-government has ever taken place. Man's history records nothing but a grim and grotesque procession of nodding waxwork figures—slowly changing in appearance, indeed, from a sponge or an echinus to a Sir Isaac Newton or a benevolent Howard—but without emancipation from the iron chain of irresistible and inexorable fate. And whither, we may well ask, is this melancholy and ludicrous procession steadily marching on? To what worthy goal, at last, are we all being sped thus helplessly along? Let there be no poetic illusions, say our new teachers who would better the lovely story of a human fall and a divine redemption. All is plain prose; and the goal we shall reach is "extinction."

"Every great thing," says Dr. Büchner, "which man has ever accomplished upon the earth, must vanish, and in the universal bosom of eternal matter be swallowed up."[1] "There approaches a time," says Frederick Strauss, "when the earth will be no longer inhabited; and then, every living and rational thing, with all its works and doings, its politics, its art, its science, shall not merely disappear and leave no trace behind, but shall have left no *memory* even of its existence behind in any spiritual being whatever. With the earth, its history too will utterly vanish away."[2]

It is obvious, however, that such melancholy notions as these simply explain nothing. They make no attempt to clear up, or to give any human and rational account of, the dreadful mysteries of moral ruin and degradation by which we are everywhere surrounded. *They deny point blank that there is any such degradation to lament.* They simply say there is no more *fall* from any high ideal, no more cause for compunction about the matter, no more hope of recovery and re-ascent, than in the degradation of a mountain, when the stones slip down from the cliff and are passively beaten into sand at its foot.

And should we bitterly complain of God's

---

[1] *Der Gottesbegriff*, p. 27.
[2] *Alte und neue Glaube*, p. 227.

injustice in exposing us to all these uncalled-for miseries, the grave reply is, There is no God to complain to, and no injustice to complain of. It is all FATE. Things are so because they are. And we must console ourselves as best we may with the reflection that any catastrophe we may complain of now is nothing when compared with the horrible catastrophe that is coming. But then happily all will soon be for ever at an end.

From all such sickly forebodings a man of sense impatiently turns away. When Job's comforters tried to drown their friend's accumulated grief in the still greater grief of finding himself a wicked hypocrite, who had brought all the trouble on his own head, they still left him hope of recovery by repentance. Here we are left no hope at all. And therefore we turn back with thankfulness and joy to the animating rational picture set before us by the Christian Church; where shame and fall, well used, point towards recovery; where the race, like the individual, is shown how it may (if it *will*) only lose its pristine animal-innocence of childhood's protected garden, to receive it back again in enhanced beauty and heightened worth; and where (as M. Lenormant well points out),[1] unlike all the other pictures of man's moral history that the world has ever seen,

---

[1] *Origines de l'Histoire*, i. 65.

Hope gilds the sombre landscape and almost simultaneously with the "fall of man" gives the promise of his redemption.

(3.) But there is a third obstacle which sometimes appears to stand in the way of Christian belief about the Fall of Man from pristine innocence; and it is probably the commonest of all. *How many persons feel an unreflecting repugnance to the story-like form in which the Hebrew prophet has seen good to couch his sublime teaching!* How many even thoughtful men there are, who cannot help indeed accepting the doctrine enshrined there, yet who resent the poetry that so eloquently teaches the inner meaning of the world's deep tragedy, just because it is poetry and not bald nineteenth-century prose. They forget, surely, that this story does not address itself to the nineteenth century only, nor to philosophers only, nor to scientific men only; but that its audience is all mankind in every age. Think then of the amazing complexity of the task! The story must be adapted to all races, to both sexes, and to all ages. The savage must be drawn by it; the little children must be pleased by it; the woman's heart must be interested and satisfied; and even the philosopher must be tempted by it to lay aside for an hour his books and his instruments, and, taking the hand of his little daughter, to

LECT. V.

listen in church to the simple yet profound and suggestive story, how the paradise of human innocence was lost and regained. With what poor success has even a Milton done this, writing for merely one people, of a certain European stock, at a very brief period of their long history! *Who shall succeed in doing it for the whole human race?* Surely then with patience—nay, with gratitude—should every reasonable man, who would have some reasonable account given to his children of the source of human sin, accept this simple childlike episode of the great Semitic poem of the origin of man. How could it be bettered? "Man emerged (it says) at fiat of divine Reason and steadfast Law from the world of dust and matter—last in point of time, first in point of dignity. He received, as the ripe fruit of many a previous development, a precious but a perilous gift—the gift of free-will and self-censure. He awoke; he became aware of intellectual primacy; he began to generalise and classify and give names to things, as no creature had ever done before. He next became conscious of the pressure of natural law, and of power either to concur, or to withhold concurrence from it. And so, amid the innocent dumb creatures, there now stood one innocent—for all too short a moment—like themselves, but (unlike them) poised on a slippery possibility of wilful fall. Behold, ye angels of heaven! Behold, ye kindred creatures that inhabit sea and land! Your master and your king is come. How perfect, how like an image of God, how transcendent a thought spoken out (as it were) and revealed to the world, stood MAN, for a brief space, upon the earth! His form, so long prepared and in the higher vertebrates foretold, is 'very good.' His mind is dominant and regnant amid beast and bird and fish. His character, as yet unsullied, shines serene in childlike simplicity, without distraction or self-conflict, 'naked and not ashamed.' But, alas, how soon will this bright scene be clouded over! Some lower instinct obeyed, some bestial memory indulged, some carnal impulse gratified, will bring with it, on reflection, shame and self-reproach. And then the endless warfare has begun. It is the FALL OF MAN. And henceforth, amid toil and bitter experience of evil, a stern selection shall commence of the morally fittest and strongest, for survival amid some future happier surroundings. But is victory, for any, henceforth possible? Is not moral survival, amid the clash of animal passions and the ever-tightening habits of greed and selfishness, a hopeless and unsubstantial dream? No: along with the fall came the animating hope of recovery—hope that always

I

makes glad and strong the heart of man, confidence that all is not lost, but that, somehow—in God's good way and time—there shall eventually come redemption."

Such, in plain paraphrase of modern prose, is the ancient Semitic parable of the origin of human sin. Who will undertake to better it? Who will deny that the special genius displayed here is a kind of divine flash of inspiration? Who will refuse to see that the whole story is bathed in a kind of dayspring from on high, and is suited to our needs, awakening to our conscience, stimulating to our brotherly love, rendering the very fall and degradation of man but the first act of a sublime drama, and promising, ere it reach its conclusion and the curtain fall, to be completed and crowned by some divine Redemption.[1]

---

[1] Cf. Lenormant, *Origines de l'Histoire*, i. 107.—"Rien n'oblige à prendre au pied de la lettre le récit du chapitre II. de la Genèse. On est en droit, sans sortir de l'orthodoxie, de le considérer comme une figure destinée à rendre sensible un fait de l'ordre purement moral. Ce n'est donc pas la forme du récit qui importe ici ; c'est le dogme qu'elle exprime. Et ce dogme de la déchéance de la race des hommes, par le mauvais usage que ses premiers auteurs ont fait de leur libre arbitre, est une vérité éternelle, qui nulle part d'ailleurs n'éclate avec la même netteté. Elle fournit la seule solution du redoubtable problème, qui revient toujours se dresser devant l'esprit de l'homme."

LECTURE VI.

REDEMPTION.

Psalm xxxi. 8: "Thou hast set my feet in a large room."

WE reach to-day a "large" and animating subject—the REDEMPTION of mankind from the consequences of the Fall. These two ideas are closely related, and are complementary to each other; and the balance of Christian doctrine would be fatally disturbed if either should be held or discussed apart from the other. The word "redemption," however, must never for a moment be regarded as a complete and adequate expression of all that is involved in the profound mystery of man's recovery from moral degradation. It is, on the face of it, a metaphorical word; and a "metaphor" is nothing more than a play of fancy, a gauzy network of analogies, thrown deftly round some delicate and fugitive idea difficult to grasp. Such ideas elude direct handling. Indeed, all truth is coy, and shy of too impetuous approach.[1] And the subtlest results of thinking seem gifted—like the ultimate atoms of matter—with a strange power of mutual repulsion, which forbids a perfect coherence. We are not, therefore, to expect a faultless logical expression, or strict mathematical accuracy, when we come to deal with such high spiritual matters as these.[2] The word "redemption" is a metaphor. Now metaphor is a kind of poetry; and all poetry appeals, of course, to the imagination rather than to the reason.

(1.) Now what is the main obstacle to Christian belief which bars the way against men of scientific training, when they are invited to approach the naturally animating and attractive subject of redemption? It is, I think, simply the fact *that, in ordinary Christian teaching, they find the whole theory of moral recovery and rehabilitation too much personified and dramatised and thrown into imaginative forms.* For this is a method which science nowadays, rather too stiffly, refuses

---

[1] Τὸν δὲ ἀληθείας ἐραστὴν εἰρηνικὸν εἶναι, κἂν ταῖς ζητήσεσι, προσῆκεν. (Clem. Alex., *Strom.* viii. 6.) "La vérité est comme les femmes capricieuses, que l'on perd pour les trop aimer." (Renan, *Essais*, p. 202.)

[2] Πεπαιδευμένου ἐστὶν ἐπὶ τοσοῦτον τἀκριβὲς ἐπιζητεῖν, ἐφ' ὅσον ἡ τοῦ πράγματος φύσις ἐπιδέχεται. (Aristotle, *Nic. Eth.* i. 4.)

to follow. It cherishes an almost irrational suspicion of that indispensable gift of imagination, by whose aid we round and shape our thoughts into "ideas," and so bring them home to our consciousness as human and intelligible. But meantime far more than half the language used by science itself is metaphor and poetry. And, whenever, leaving our arid investigations, we try to teach other people and to put them in possession of our results, then to abandon metaphor is to abandon all hope of success, and refusal to dramatise the subject is nothing else than refusal to interest and instruct. If then the representations, by which Christian teachers endeavour to reach men with the conviction that their moral imperfection is remediable, seem to people of culture crude and scarcely tolerable, let it be remembered that they are all confessedly incomplete and inadequate. But meanwhile the fact, the reality, intended to be presented remains. It is that—contrary to all reasonable expectations—the accelerating velocity of human downfall may be, and in millions of cases actually has been, arrested; that the accumulating tension of evil habits need not enchain with a hopeless degradation; that the sinful soul may (so to speak) be "pardoned," and the captive victim be bought off and "redeemed." If you wish to understand

and to grasp the idea of some great building, some castle or cathedral, you naturally walk round it and view it from many different points; till at last the stereoscopic notion of it dawns upon you and you have embraced its meaning as a whole. And so it is with this great mystery of the moral re-instatement of man. Viewed from one side it is "recovery" or "regeneration" or "renewal" or "conversion" or "redemption;" viewed from another side it is "atonement" or "justification" or "forgiveness" or "sanctification" or "adoption" or "salvation." But not one of these expressions, nor all of them together, are full and adequate descriptions of that strange thing, the reversal of man's fall. Still less is any one bound to receive as satisfactory any of the (so called) "schemes of salvation"—whether forensic or otherwise—by which good men have often aided themselves and helped their own generation, but which they have thereupon been tempted to regard as adequate conceptions and to call "the Gospel." But the Divine Gospel of God's good news is a larger and sublimer thing than any of our "schemes" or "plans of salvation." The ways of God are grander and more comprehensive and more loving (we may be sure) than anything which we are likely to attribute to Him. And therefore no man need stumble or "be offended" at the mere temporary expedients or word-pictures of theologians; no man need build obstacles to his faith out of mere metaphors or out of the simple language of the Bible. He should rather ask himself one home question: "Do I desire, by aid of Christ, to disembarrass my soul from clinging sins and from the power of evil habits, rashly formed perhaps in days of my ignorance? If so, I surely shall not stumble, on the threshold of my inquiries after that salvation, by reason of its too pictorial language or too traditional method of presentment. Rather, if thousands have already found emancipation and serenity through the agency of belief in Christ, I too will approach that I may see Him for myself. I will 'become a fool that I may be wise;' and will try to learn how it can possibly be that One, who died eighteen hundred years ago in a far-off land, should be to thousands here and now so great a benefactor."

(2.) But at this point another obstacle to Christian belief suddenly starts into view. *To many men it seems absolutely impossible that the course of moral degradation, once entered upon, should ever be reversed.* The thought of such reversal may indeed be enchanting, and the good news of such a hope (if it were only true) would be arresting and delightful. It would be news to make a man look up with a new interest from

LECT. VI.

his weary ledger; to make a woman pause in her round of dreary gaieties; to make a youth—sliding morally downwards and letting himself go—stop and recover a joyous energy; to make a child—often so much more sad and thoughtful than we have any idea of—feel bright and confident about his young life. But then is such recovery within the order of things? Only look around! Here is a world crowded with a thousand millions of human beings, every one of them fallen from his ideal state. Evil, bitter physical and moral evil, slipping in like some lithe intruder, has fixed its poisonous fangs upon each individual of them. Not one has escaped. The very baby in the cradle is passionate;[1] the very grey-beard, with one foot in the grave, is miserly; the streets are filled with troops of harlots, doomed to a bestial life and an early death; drunkenness, murder, hatred, lust, fraud, and horrible war steep the world to the lips in misery. How can all this torrent of wickedness be ever stayed and its downward course be reversed?

And again, if we look to individual lives, how does every heart conceal a lurking traitor within, and every conscience feel that

"Not e'en the dearest heart, and next our own,
Knows half the reasons why we smile or sigh."

[1] St. Augustine, *Confess.* i. 11.

We are all of us like people wounded in some fray against the enemies of our peace—staggering under various temptations, stumbling, falling, rising again, hoping against hope, and fighting a battle which is all but irretrievably lost. And meanwhile every failure weakens our character and disarms our future resistance. The habit of defeat begins to grow upon us. We are every day more discouraged than before. Defensive power wanes, in proportion as the aggressive power of appetite and passion waxes ever stronger by habitual indulgence. In short, recovery of balance and quiet self-control becomes daily more hopeless; until, like St. Paul, we cry out in despair, "Who shall deliver me from the bondage of this death?"[1]

And yet, on the other hand, if the assurance of redemption and deliverance seem too *good* news to be true, the reverse of that assurance is far too *bad* news to be true. It is really impossible for any sane man to sit down tranquilly in view of the enormous moral evils which both history and experience reveal to him, without cherishing some hope and framing some theory of their ultimate extirpation. It seems part of our very nature to rise in revolt against this degrading reign of moral chaos and brutal impulse amid which we live.

[1] *Romans* vii. 24.

And—what is more striking still—the better the man, the purer, the nobler, the more he be truly and ideally a son of man and a scion of the human race, the more intense is always his repugnance and hatred against this special class of evils. Physical pain he may patiently bear. The spectacle of Nature's universal warfare he may endure to witness, under the impression that it is, in the end, beneficent. But what can he say, what can he do, in presence of the appalling fact of almost universal moral degradation? No possible good, it seems, can come of that. "*Corruptio optimi pessima.*" And to be finally assured of the hopeless shipwreck of that "last result of time," humanity, would indeed extinguish all respect for Nature and her ways, and destroy all interest in an evolution which has issued, it would seem, in a total and disastrous failure of that one race, in whom its preparation, for a million years, had found its end and culmination.

We are, therefore, it seems, in "a strait betwixt two." Both alternatives are equally impossible and unthinkable—both that of man's redemption and recovery, and that of his irremediable fall. And yet, is there not one element in the latter of the two alternatives, which makes it even more unthinkable than the former? There are, no doubt, many astonishing things in the universe, and "Nature (as Professor Tyndall says) is full of anomalies, which no foresight can predict, and which experiment alone can reveal."[1] But there is only one absolutely *shocking* anomaly in the universe; and that is the assurance (if we are really compelled to feel the assurance) that we are witnessing a moral degradation which it is beyond the power, or beside the will, of God to stay in its downward course to final ruin. We are no doubt aroused, for instance, to feel a certain surprise when we are first told that Uranus rotates the wrong way; or that transparent ammonia actually intercepts 5,000 times more heat than equally transparent air[2]; or that the same atoms, differently hooked together into molecules, may be now an acid and now an alkali[3]; or that an orchid sets a spring-gun for a bee[4]; or that a human being may possess a double consciousness.[5] But none of these surprises are "shocking," repugnant, or such as a man *ought* not to believe. Now a man ought not to believe that the unnatural, reeking degradation of the slums in some great city is part of Nature's order, need not therefore be interfered with, and cannot be redeemed.

[1] *Lecture on Heat*, p. 86.
[2] Tyndall, *Radiation*, p. 16.
[3] Cooke, *New Chemistry*, p. 249.
[4] Darwin, *Fertilization of Orchids*, p. 222.
[5] Carpenter, *Mental Physiology*, p. 460.

LECT. VI.

(3.) But not only are we able to see, on steady reflection, that some possibility of human redemption must certainly exist; *we are also able to understand, in some measure, through what avenue it may be expected to come.* Improved economical conditions would not bring it;[1] easy and pleasant environment, with absence of poverty and toil, would not secure it. For lazy abundance seems usually to degrade and to prove a Capua to human virtue;[2] and there is many a lovely and delicious scene where "only man is vile."[3] Nor does increase of knowledge insure moral elevation; nor the highest dignity of personal surroundings engender it;[4] nor the perfection of political institutions guarantee

---

[1] This may be seen in our own well-to-do colonies, and in the United States. Read Nordhoff's *Communistic Societies in the United States*, p. 292.

[2] See Trollope's *West Indies:* and *South Sea Bubbles*, by "The Earl and the Doctor," 3rd edit., 1872.

[3] See Andrew Wilson, *Travels in Cashmir*, &c., 1875, p. 225, &c. Hunter, *Orissa*, 1872, i. 118, &c. De Carné, *Indo-China*, 1872, p. xviii. &c. White, *Land Journey from Asia*, 1871, p. 2, &c. De Beauvoir, *Voyage*, 1870, ii. 168, 198, &c. Tozer, *Turkey*, 1869, ii. 28. Reville, *Peuples non-civilizés*, 1883, ii. 81.

[4] "Louis XV., by his noble carriage and the mild, yet majestic, expression of his features, was worthy to succeed to Louis the Great." (Mme. de Campan, *Life of Marie Antoinette*, i. 14.) Yet read her description of this man's heartless and diabolical immoralities, in the same volume; and his treason against children, subjects of his paternal government.

it.[1] Not even can philosophy, or familiarity with the sublimest thoughts and maxims of conduct, give renovation of character. The very height to which a thinker or an orator is often borne by strength of intellectual pinion, or by the fervour of excitement, forms a peril from which many do not escape unscathed. No; the experience of the world's history, and the accumulated knowledge we now possess of all sorts and conditions of human character, have rendered the position unassailable—that *religion* is by far the most powerful factor within our reach for effecting permanent moral changes. It was the sanction of religion which first restrained the casual impulses of primæval savagery, and reduced them under the yoke of law; it was religion which welded roving desert-tribes into a nation; it was religion which tamed and transformed the barbarous hordes that broke into the Roman Empire. It is religion, it is Christianity — no candid observer will dispute the statement— which is at this day binding together, as with a subtle chemical affinity, the civilised peoples of the earth, and redeeming them from the intolerable scourge of perpetual war. And if a yet

---

[1] For France, see Dauban, *Le Fond de la Société*, &c., 1873; p. 36 : Greg, *Essays*, 2nd series ; p. 31. For England, " Circumspice ! "

LECT. VI.

further redemption is to be looked for, and some relief is to be expected from the present crushing evil of pauperism—with its twin attendants, crime and disease—there seems no doubt that here too the angel of deliverance will take the form of "religion." For even the most advanced reformer and outspoken advocate of social change that modern England has given ear to, confesses this truth in plain words. "There is," says he, "a gospel of selfishness—soothing as soft flutes to those who, having fared well themselves, think that every body ought to be satisfied; but the salvation of society, the hope for the free full development of humanity, is in the Gospel of Brotherhood, the GOSPEL OF CHRIST."[1]

(4.) But if so, and if it be conceded that through religion alone moral transformations of any permanence and value are to be looked for, *can we understand by what process these singular conversions are effected?* It seems that we can. In the first place, we have to inquire which of the mental powers is the most readily and universally accessible to exterior influence; which is the most plastic and impressionable and likely (as it were) to hold the door open for the entrance of the new guest, who is in time to become master of the house. The answer to that inquiry may

[1] H. George, *Social Problems*, p. 9.

be reached in a very simple and pleasant way. If any one will go into—that most practical of all schools for the study of human nature—his own children's nursery, he will there see the human powers and feelings at work, with that curious suggestiveness which always accompanies the origins and embryo-stages of things, and without the remotest attempt at affectation or disguise.[1] And the very first thing he will there discover is this:—*That the earliest and most universal mental power to awaken into activity is the imagination.* This power, if he watch long enough, will soon be followed by a slowly developing reason, and this again by a gradually maturing conscience. Of course they all three ultimately combine and are intertwined together. But their start is not simultaneous: just as, in many plants, the stamens and the pistil do not awake to action together, though they appear together afterwards.[2] The pictorial imagination then, will be the commonest and the most widely-spread and the most childlike in its easy sensitiveness to new impressions, of all the faculties belonging to the human family.

If he then go forth into the streets among the

---

[1] See Reville, *Peuples non-civilisés*, ii. 223.
[2] Lubbock, *Flowers in Relation to Insects* (*Nature* Series), p. 30.

LECT. VI.

masses of mankind, he will there find his first conclusions abundantly verified. For while nine-tenths of our race are arrested at various early stages of their mental growth, there is one stage which they seem, almost without any exception, to have reached, and that is the stage of imaginative impressibility. Tell either your children or the populace a *story*, and you are quite sure to be listened to. Garnish your public speech well with *illustrations* drawn from tangible and visible things, and you will attract men as Orpheus attracted the wild denizens of the forest with his lyre. Invite universal mankind to dramatic *representations* and you will charm them all. Not only will the educated and half-educated go in crowds to see a play of Shakespeare acted on the stage, but the wildest street-Arab will be held entranced by the adventures of *Cinderella*, and the *blasé* London rake will be found in tears before a miracle-play at Ammergau.[1]

It is clear, therefore, that if you desire to preach the good news of redemption to all alike — to poor and rich, young and old, male and female, workman and philosopher—the one receptive organ which they all have in common, and to which you must address yourself, is the imagina-

[1] This was a fact, witnessed and recorded by a visitor at the "play," some years ago.

tion. Make your first approach there, and you will be welcomed with interest and attention. But approach directly by way of the conscience, and you make your appeal to the very organ which is, perhaps, at present paralysed by inaction and darkened by sin. Or approach directly by the intellect, and you are instantly obliged to adapt yourself to a hundred different classes of mind and degrees of civilisation. Your treatise on the Gospel composed for the twelfth century will be consigned to oblivion in the sixteenth century: and your "body of divinity" carefully elaborated for the Reformation period will be impatiently torn up and thrown away when a new reformation-period begins to dawn upon the world. Only that abides which—like Homer, like Shakespeare, and (above all) like the Bible—appeals to the universally receptive power, the imagination. And through that, therefore, must come the first pictured traits of the new and redeeming Ideal, which is to dissolve gradually away the old worldly notions and sensual conceptions of life, and to replace the old Adam, the old type of human nature, with a new and a better one.

(4.) But a further question here arises. *With what new Ideal, precisely, shall the receptive imagination be supplied, if the whole man is to be thereby*

K

gradually leavened and redeemed? The right soil has been found: with what seed shall it be sown? The new Ideal to be presented before it must (as we long ago found out) be something distinctively human, else it will find no sympathy and no welcome from the ordinary human mind. It must be something attractive and simple, else it will not come home to all alike. Yet it must be profound and mysterious, lest it be despised and seem to challenge fathoming to the bottom. Again, it must present the character of gentleness and peace, or it will (as the Old Testament is said to have done among the Goths and Maories) stir up and inflame the very lower passions that it was meant to hush to rest. Nor must it fail to carry marks of suffering and brave endurance, else it will not correspond to the experience of the vast majority of the human race. Nay, it should—if that were possible—show signs of having met, and known how to conquer, that last and most terrible enemy of the whole human species, Death. Surely it were no vain dream to believe that, if such an ideal figure could be projected powerfully and continuously on the imagination, a new type (as it were) of mankind might in course of long centuries be gradually engendered. The supreme beauty of such a heavenly character would enkindle sympathy and loving adoration. The lips of such a SON OF MAN, parted with words of welcome for the sinful and of restoration for the fallen, would awaken hope and earnest purpose in many a despairing soul. And as each individual came under its transforming influence, some—many, it may be; all, it might have been hoped—would fall in love and be melted into conformity with this ideal man. They would see in Him a glorified image of their own possible better selves; would feel convinced that this was the idea of God, existent from the beginning, concerning the human species; and so by loyalty and self-devotion would be elevated, regenerated, renewed in the spirit of their minds —in a word, would be redeemed.

And then all that is wanting is some organisation by means of which the redeeming figure may be (so to speak) perpetually dramatised to men's imagination and may be set forth visibly before their eyes. Now sacred art in its various branches, the tranquil ritual of the Church, saintly imitations of Christ's life (in multifarious partial ways and imperfect degrees), and the rhetorical or descriptive presentation of the subject by Christian teachers, have certainly succeeded in keeping alive for more than eighteen centuries a most vivid and heart-transforming "remembrance" of such a living and energising ideal, in the person of JESUS CHRIST. And in those who fully receive it, this new conception seems to cast out and take the place of all previously existing ones, whatever they may have been—heathenish, Pharisaic, Sadducee, worldly, carnal, devilish, or any other. Its recipients appear to live henceforth as if born into new surroundings and gradually awakening to new sensibilities. To the old life and views of things they have bidden adieu. They say, "I feel (as it were) crucified with Christ, to whom my heart's allegiance is now given. Nevertheless I live; I am more fully and consciously alive than I ever was before. Yet it seems no longer I, but Christ who liveth in me."[1]

This, then, is the redemption, through JESUS, the world's Saviour, which is committed to the Church's keeping from age to age. This is the Gospel of good news—at least, in one of its many aspects—which has brought peace, courage, and strength to the untold thousands of the human race. And this is a Christianity to which science, so far from being hostile or indifferent, ought to be most friendly. For it thwarts (so far as I am aware) no single scientific advance, it traverses no single scientific position. It teaches, as science also does, that no creature and no species is fixed in an invariable state; but that all things are

---

[1] *Galatians* ii. 20.

moulded by incessant change and plastic to the
constant touch of external influences.[1] It acknowledges, with science, the fact of occasional
counter-evolution; and sees in human degradation one of the saddest examples of its occurrence.[2]
Yet it believes, with science, that exterior and
more cosmic agencies may, in a marked way,
alter many things—as oscillations in the earth's
orbit probably produced the glacial epochs, with
all their vast results,[3] and as the great lunar tide-wave daily reverses the rivers' downward course—

> "And hushes half the babbling Wye,
> And makes a silence in the hills."

Yet withal it bows the head, with science, to the
majesty of unbroken and invariable Law; and holds
it to be as firm and invariable as the eternal
"Amen," of whose standing will Law is the expression. And it perceives, as science also does, that
the way in which the law of variation works is by
the unexpected, yet from all eternity prepared, appearance—"Epiphany" is the Greek word for it
—of some exterior agent, some divergent force,
some new strain, in the animal sphere some

---

[1] "We strain our imagination to conceive the processes of creation; while, in reality, they are round us daily."—(Duke of Argyll, *Unity of Nature*, 1884; p. 270.) Cf. Darwin, *Earthworms*, 1881; p. 258: Grant Allen, *Colours of Flowers*, 1882; p. 20.   [2] *Unity of Nature*, p. 372.
[3] See Croll, *Climate and Time*, 1875; pp. 77, 325.

fresh departure, among mankind some dazzling "genius" who turns the world upside down.

The scientific obstacles, therefore, to Christian belief seem, in this department of religious thought, remarkably few. One glance around at the state of our great modern cities, one hour's reflection on the teaching of the world's history, one earnest effort of the will to revive belief in the general beneficence of Nature, and to reënkindle hope in the future of its crowning result, Man—these mental acts, of which all thoughtful men are capable, seem to be enough for a complete recovery of the Christian point of view about redemption. And though at times, when the better feelings ebb, it is possible to surrender to more despairing thoughts, and almost to make shipwreck of one's faith—at such times, by recourse to the aids of the Church, and by bending the proud knee in prayer, and sacrificing one hour to quiet meditation over the Gospel page, a marvellous recovery is possible. And the grey-haired philosopher goes back to his microscope or his laboratory a serener and a better man; because he has learnt what that saying of the great Master meant—"I thank Thee, Father, that Thou hast hidden these things from the wise and prudent, and hast revealed them unto babes."[1]

[1] *Matthew* xi. 25.

LECTURE VII.

IMMORTALITY.

Rom. vi. 23 : "The gift of God is eternal life."

THERE is hardly any subject more personally interesting to all of us, and at the same time more impatient of scientific handling, than the subject of "a future life." And its great and baffling difficulty is, perhaps, the cause of a very curious phenomenon, which has lately presented itself in the world of thought. There is in the air a kind of second "renaissance," a second revival of a long bygone way of thinking. But the renaissance, this time, is not (like that of the fifteenth century) a mere revival of the pagan classical way of thinking—though even that has, in some quarters, been feebly attempted—but rather a rehabilitation of Oriental, of Hindu, ways of viewing the world and of estimating human life. For this the studies of half a century have formed a steady preparation. Lassen, Weber, Muir, Max Müller, Hardy, Williams, and a host of others, have not laboured in vain. Their works have created a widely spread interest in Indian affairs, and have fostered an evergrowing taste for Indian studies. And Buddhism, above all, has been found to harmonise so strangely with many of the most favourite speculations of modern science that something more than sympathy has been expressed for it; and our Missions to the East, and even our (apparently) secure and long-established English Christianity, have been threatened by a reflex wave of aggression from that quarter.[1] We can afford to smile at the audacity

[1] The singular curiosity about Buddhism which is felt nowadays is shown by the great number of books which are constantly written on that subject. Such interest is not surprising, when we remember two things—(1) that Buddhism, at this moment, counts many more adherents than any other religion on the face of the earth ; (2), that it offers salvation by the way of the pure intellect, a way much affected by a "scientific age" In December, 1872, *Good Words* printed an abstract of a Buddhist sermon. In 1875 an attack on Christianity, called *An Exposition of Error*, was published in Japan, its objections being oddly similar to those of Celsus in the second century. In 1881 public lectures were held at Tokio, in support of Buddhism. A year or two ago, the Bishop of Tinnivelly in South India was astonished by the apparition of a Buddhist counter-mission from Ceylon, which held a meeting in a Hindu temple, and made overtures for an offensive alliance against Christianity with the Brahmins. And at the present moment, in London, any one may procure at Mudie's library a strange attempt, by a Mr. Sinnett, to adapt

of this Quixotic enterprise. But still we should remember what such phenomena always indicate. They invariably presuppose a restless and growing dissatisfaction with existing forms of belief. They express a dangerous tension between older and newer religious ideas. And they herald an earnest endeavour, on the part of serious and thoughtful men, to crystallise afresh their conceptions of human destiny and duty amid the changed surroundings of the times.[1]

But why should we always thus go backwards in our researches after truth ? Interesting as history may be, indispensable as a knowledge of the past is, both for understanding the present

Buddhism to the English taste. But when Englishmen shall begin to sit still and pine languidly, in Buddhist fashion, after annihilation, a good many things besides English Christianity will be drawing towards their end.

[1] "At the present moment, unbelief in the revelation of the unseen is undergoing, here as elsewhere, a shock which is without parallel, at least in the history of this country, for the activity of its manifestations."—(Right Hon. W. E. Gladstone, in *Contemporary Review*, October 1878.) "It is no secret that among the educated men of France and Italy, with the exception of a few individuals, the Christian dogma has ceased to hold an authoritative sway."—(*Ibid.*) An intelligent traveller, lately come from Spain, reports that the same phenomenon is still more remarkably prominent there. While "the Germans have outgrown their faith, they have become entirely indifferent to religious forms. They neither accept nor reject any theological creed ; they simply pay no attention to such things."—(C. Hillebrand, in *Nineteenth Century*, June, 1880.)

LECT. VII.

and preparing for the future, yet surely it is childish to be so often engaged in "reviving" some bygone period or other. It is ludicrous to be so perpetually engaged, as some are, in "beating back the spirit of the age," and in trying timidly to float, by a slender backwater, in opposition to the mighty stream of Divine progress in the world.[1] Above all, why should we have recourse to ancient Indian speculations for aid amid the perplexities of modern Europe? Rather, while we acknowledge that hazy poetic mysticism is the special privilege of the East, as clear scientific thinking forms the prerogative of the West, we should perceive that there is a central point, midway between the two, where has arisen a power able to hold them both in equipoise, and to combine both East and West in harmony. And that power is CHRISTIANITY.[2]

[1] Five-and-thirty years ago, when we were in the red heat of our Romanticism, and some of us were set upon restoring the "Ages of Faith," a singular warning reached us from an unexpected quarter. Mr. Pugin, a recent convert to Romanism, wrote as follows:—"All anterior to the Reformation is described as a sort of Utopia—pleasant meadows, happy peasants, merry England, cheap bread and beef for nothing, all holy monks, all holy priests, all holy everybody. I once believed in Utopia myself. But, when tested by stern facts of history, it all melts away like a dream."—(Pugin, *Earnest Address*, 1850.)

[2] Christianity was, by its origin, an Oriental religion; but by St. Paul (practically) and by St. John (theoretically) it

Take, for instance, the subject which claims our especial attention in the present lecture, the difficult subject of "Immortality." The East has here always tended to lose itself amid a mist of impracticable and immoral theories. In Brahminism it has dreamed of universal absorption in a Pantheistic deity.[1] In Buddhism it has pointed on, beyond a long purgatory of innumerable transmigrations, towards a Nirwana-heaven of dreamless swoon.[2] In Parsism, Gnosticism, Manichæanism, it has indulged itself in other bewildering speculations. While the West has ever been tempted to lose itself in hard scientific denials. Christianity alone seems able to maintain the balance between them, and to satisfy all the requirements of the problem. And this she does by carefully and steadily insisting on three things.

was adapted to the requirements of the west. And thus eastern and western ideas became happily welded together. But three centuries before, the way had been providentially prepared by the sweeping conquests of Alexander.

Hence arose a widespread use of the Greek language in the East, and eventually the translation of the Old Testament into that tongue. Jesus Himself seems to have used both an Asiatic and a European language. For instance in Matthew xv. 8, He cites the LXX where it differs from the Hebrew; while in Matthew xxvii. 46, He cites the Hebrew where it differs from the LXX (cf. Grindfield, *Apology for LXX*, p. 185.) "La theorie Chrétienne n'est rien que la religion primitive des Aryens."—(E. Burnouf, *Science des Religions*, 3rd edit., p. 114.)

[1] Cf. Monier Williams, *Hinduism*, p. 51.
[2] Cf. Bishop Titcomb, *Chapters on Buddhism*, pp. 34, 58.

First, for men trained and able to philosophise on these high matters—great liberty of speculation. *Next*, for men of science and history—strong and definite appeal to facts. *Lastly*, for busy people of little taste for theory, who want truth stamped with authority and wrapped up in some tangible and striking form—a vivid and artistic presentation.[1] And it may be well, therefore, to consider this question of Immortality successively from these three points of view.

(1.) First, then, viewing it as a subject for *speculation*, let it never be forgotten by those who have any difficulties about the matter, that this is precisely one of those points—such as the Divine Nature, the time of the world's end, the origin of evil, and several other mysterious questions—which Christianity expressly declines

---

[1] It is surely quite remarkable how readily the leading facts of the Gospel lend themselves to artistic treatment. Hence, exclaims Ewald, "Elevate Christ as high as you can, but whatever you do, blur not and darken not His earthly history, lest you destroy the only bridge which can lead you to His heaven and His eternity."—(*Christus und Seine Zeit*, p. xii.) "This conception of God, which is the child's, is evidently the only one which can be universal; and therefore for us is the only one which can be true."—(Ruskin, *Modern Painters*, iv. 87.) "Even purgatory, taken as a symbolic representation, has its meaning, like everything else which gifted souls from the beginning have seen by intuition, and then have expressed in earthly speech."—(Tieck, *Schutzgeist*, p. 55.)

to reduce into definite terms of the human understanding.¹ It therefore leaves us perfectly free to speculate upon the "how," "when," and "where" of the future life, as much as we please and as far as we can. Indeed we cannot go far. Our faculties are not adapted for a thorough comprehension of these unseen verities. And in making this confession we are standing on similar ground with that of scientific men, who often feel bound to record their absolute ignorance, in detail, about scientific truths. Thus Mr. Herbert Spencer makes a general confession of the most sweeping kind. He says, "The man of science more than any other truly *knows* that in its ultimate essence nothing can be known."² Again, "How physical forces can transform themselves into intellectual (says Dr. Büchner) is inexplicable; but not more inexplicable after all than the conversion of one physical force into another."³ Dr. Grove confesses, "We have *no* knowledge as to the exact nature of any mode

---

¹ "The Christian religion, as its Founder taught it, employs itself very little with dreams and anxious speculations about the future life. Rather it fixes our attention on a great building in this world, at which all generations must work; until He returns, who shall bring His reward with Him."—(Flügge, *Der Himmel der Zukunft*, p. 328.)

² H. Spencer, *First Principles*, p. 66.

³ Büchner, *Lumière et Vie*, French trans. p. 166.

LECT. VII.

of chemical action."[1] Faraday said, "He once thought he knew something about electricity; but the more he investigated it, the less he found he understood it."[2] Dr. Bastian asks, "Why should oxygen unite with hydrogen to form water? and what do we know concerning the actual phenomena of nutrition? They are still inscrutable mysteries."[3] Professor Tyndall declares, "Between molecular mechanics and consciousness is interposed a fissure, over which the ladder of physical reasoning is incompetent to carry us."[4] And even Professor Haeckel writes as follows:—"What do we know certainly of the essential nature of *matter* and of *force*; what of *gravitation*; of the essential nature of *electricity* or of the *imponderables* generally, whose very existence is not proved; what of the *ether*, upon which our formal science of light and optics is founded; and what of the *atomic* theory, on which our chemistry is built? *Yet are we to cease to teach these sciences because we do not certainly know these things?*"[5] Certainly not, replies the Christian:

[1] Grove, *Correlation of Forces*, 2nd edit., p. 85.
[2] See *Quarterly Review*, January 1877.
[3] Bastian, *Beginnings of Life*, i. 55.
[4] Prof. Tyndall, in *Nineteenth Century*, November, 1878, p. 68.
[5] Haeckel, *Freie Wissenschaft*, p. 55. Cf. Virchow, *Freedom of Science*, 2nd edit., p. 20: "*All* human knowledge is but fragmentary."

only then you should have some sympathy with the Church, which persists (on very high authority) in teaching truths which she makes no pretensions logically to understand; but rather has plainly stated, from the very beginning, to be things "which eye hath not seen nor ear heard, neither hath it entered into the heart of man to conceive:" and you should listen to Mr. H. Spencer, when he says, "In religion let us recognise the high merit, that from the beginning it has dimly discerned [an] ultimate verity, and has never ceased to insist on it . . . . each higher creed rejecting the definite interpretations previously given."[1]

Acknowledging, then, the inaccessibility of those realities which death alone can fully reveal, the Church has nevertheless always faithfully taught the lesson which Christ has put into her mouth. She has proclaimed these truths: (*a*) that the present aspect of things will some day pass away, as surely as previous "dispensations" or "formations" have passed away: (*b*) that the apparent stability and reality of the world is, therefore, illusive, and the true "realities" are things neither visible nor tangible: (*c*) that man—summit though he seem of all creation, and the last result of time—still as he began only yesterday,

[1] *First Principles*, p. 97.

so to-morrow he and all his works will end; but *not without leaving effects behind* of a very permanent, and to himself deeply important, kind. For (says Christianity) not only is the human race building up—as corals build up a continent beneath the sea—a spiritual world, hidden at present and unimaginable to the builders, but a great process of *selection* is also tacitly going on, so that each individual, according to his quality, will be built in or be rejected from the great building which is growing silently beneath the temporary veil of sense. Thus, according to Christian teaching, in some mysterious way each man is immortal, and that not by any arbitrary decree of God, but, simply by the working of a certain law which is traceable throughout the universe. This law provides that all material, which lends itself to the purposes of the great Power that shapes our ends and harmonises all things, is destined to be preserved from retrograde dissolution and is privileged to "come up higher." But all material which proves recalcitrant and incompatible sinks into lower, and perhaps amorphous, conditions and goes to (what we call) "waste."

But the "dispensation" of the future, the long hoped-for "kingdom of heaven" upon earth, the "reign of angels" (so to speak) which shall one day supersede the present reign of man on this planet, is characterised by a very perplexing and subtle attribute. It is called " spirituality." The word cannot, of course, indicate anything supernatural; else it would mean something outside the great Cosmos of all-embracing law and order —in other words, outside the area of the Divine will, which finds its expression in order and law. But though it be nothing, strictly speaking, supernatural, yet the words " eternal " or " spiritual " life do constitute a pretension to belong to some higher state of things than we are, most of us, familiar with amid our temporal and worldly occupations. So the phrase " spiritual-mindedness," used by St. Paul,[1] is not unintelligible; yet it is only partly intelligible. And therefore the quality, as we know it now, seems to be merely a first streak of some coming dawn, some rising " dayspring from on high," which is to us as unintelligible now as the advent of Man and of his reign must have been to the gigantic brutes that lorded it in the forests and marshes of the Tertiary epoch. If then, in spite of their crass ignorance, the incredible and unthinkable reign of Man has, nevertheless, become an accomplished fact, there seems no reason on the face of it to deny that Man's reign, too, may very likely have to give place to something better, although some-

[1] *Romans* viii. 6.

thing now unthinkable to him. At the same time, it is clear that the new ruler of the coming age will not be abruptly created for the occasion; but will be developed, by some kind of selection, from the older stock. And everything indicates that the *principle* of selection will be the survival of those morally and intelligently most in accord with the Mind that sways the Universe;[1] while the *mechanism* of selection will probably be something finer and more spiritual than at present. It will be by discipleship, not sonship; by moral, not sexual, hereditary; by re-generation, not generation.

But whenever, hitherto, a new class of beings has been ushered into the world, not only have new climates and surroundings—a "new heaven and a new earth"—been prepared for them, but also (if observation is to be trusted) a new idea has rather abruptly budded forth from the parent stock, and a leading specimen has appeared.[2]

---

[1] "It is becoming evident that the strongest and the fittest [to survive] are not physical, nor even intellectual, strength; but moral forces."—(McCosh, *Christianity and Positivism:* 1871, p. 70.)

[2] "In the Northern Seas a remarkable variety of the common guillemot is found. It often pairs with the common kind, yet intermediate gradations have never been seen. Nor is this surprising. For variations which appear suddenly are either transmitted unaltered or not at all."—(Darwin, *Descent of Man*, 2nd Edition, p. 424.) Polymorphism, in insect larvæ, may be the origin of new species. (D'Herculais, *Les Insectes*, p. 45.) "The original tree from which all the copper-beeches in

Now just in this way—silently, abruptly, and yet (in fact) after long preparation—the second Adam, or type and fountain-head of a new race, appeared in the world. And on that type millions of the human family have since moulded their characters. They have become, by regeneration and renewal, mysteriously one with Him, and "conformed to His likeness." And attaching themselves to His side—as crystals in process of formation, by some wonderful polarity, range themselves beside a crystal already formed—they "grow up to Him in all things," extend (as it were) His incarnation, become part of his ever-expanding Body "the Church," and (to change the metaphor) are built up as living stones to form a temple for the living God.

Nor do such transformed persons live to themselves alone. Their discipleship takes effect on others too; and the spiritual heredity is passed on. They often succeed in radiating on all around them an elevation of thought and an unselfishness of heart, which enkindles a similar heat and

---

Europe have been derived was found by accident in a wood in Germany about ninety years ago."—(Coleman, *Our Heaths*, &c. p. 24.) "A short time ago a few gilled salamanders, at Paris, unexpectedly crept out from the water on to the dry land, from amid hundreds of these animals; they lost their gills and changed themselves into tritons, which breathe only through lungs."—(Haeckel, *History of Creation*, i. 241.)

vitality in many other persons. Thus they leaven the world, as yeast permeates the dough, by a rapid fecundity of spiritual life; and they engender —by a mystery as inscrutable as that of ordinary birth [1]—many spiritual sons and daughters for the unseen world. And, again, just as plant-life seizes on the lower world of dead matter and vitalises it, and as the yet higher animal-life seizes on the plant world and elevates it to a higher stage of being, while at every transformation much material is rejected as unsuitable and irreceptive, so (once more) does spiritual life seize on such animal life as is suitable, and assimilate and elevate it. And as the lower earthy compounds are dissolved and (in St. Paul's sense of the word) "die" before they can go to form the plant, and the gaseous molecules of the air are dashed to pieces by the yellow light waves [2] before they can be breathed-in by the leaves,— and as (once more) the plant-cell is disintegrated and its life is sacrificed, before its elected parts can be promoted to build up the animal or the

---

[1] "He who has, with the slightest attention, remarked the procedure with which nature, in this life, brings out and makes provision for a new being, must think himself a perfect fool if he attempts to guess how she will bring that being into another life."—(Flügge, *Himmel der Zukunft*, p. 320.)

[2] "Every ray has its proper chemical function,—the yellow in the decomposition of carbonic acid."—(Draper, *Scientific Memoirs*, 1878: p. 785.)

man,—so, it may be, the higher spiritual or "eternal" life must seize and mortify and supersede that lower life of which it takes possession, utilising its material, transforming it, and in the transition destroying it.

Now, of such mysterious transformations of force even Nature gives abundant types and hints. Dr. Büchner, whom we heard just now confess the baffling mystery of the commonest chemical changes, thus describes for us one instance of Protean transitions of force,—and that in a not very elaborate molecule. He says:—"I take some 'sulphur of antimony' and first of all *electrify* it: but this electric force instantly reveals another, that of *magnetism;* but this again presently displays another force, viz. *heat;* the heat glows into redness and presently starts the vibrations of *light;* meanwhile the mass dilates, and shows *mechanical* motion: and the diorama ends by the appearance on the scene of the *chemical* force of decomposition."[1] Here we have no less than six forces passing into and succeeding each other. And still more curious cases are reported by other chemists, such as the interchange of atoms between sodium and water—where the self-same atoms, merely hooked together under a different grouping,

---

[1] Büchner, *Lumière*, &c., p. 202.

LECT. VII.

suddenly develop quite new and unexpected qualities.[1] So that even "matter," it seems, and that in its deadest and all but primitive simplicity, is capable of putting forth the most astonishing latent powers—powers that may have lain dormant and unsuspected for perhaps a thousand millenniums. How much more, if there exist something besides matter in the universe, if there be "spirit,"—akin to God, who is a Spirit—then who shall presume to say, before experience, what latent powers it may not possess and may not, some day, amid a suitable environment, suddenly display?

(2) But Christianity not only indulges us with all these curious *speculations* about the baffling subject of Immortality: it also offers our tottering footsteps the most solid assistance that could possibly be given by presenting us with a great typical and illustrative *fact*. It assures us that its Founder, JESUS CHRIST, actually, visibly, and tangibly rose from the dead. Thus it comes armed with a definite proof that not only was He the type and germ of a new and better race to come, and in Word represented God's thought of what humanity ought to be, but also that He

[1] Cooke, *The New Chemistry*, 4th Edition, p. 252. "The qualities and chemical relations of a compound are determined fully as much by the structure of its molecules as by the nature of the atoms of which the molecules consist."—(*Ibid.* p. 249.)

overcame and survived death, and, visibly to chosen witnesses, assumed immortal life. The evidence for the truth of this reassuring fact is such as no candid inquirer can possibly treat with indifference. There is first the undoubted historical fact that, immediately after the crushing defeat and disappointment of the Crucifixion, at any rate *some event* happened which suddenly imparted a joyful animation and expansion to the dismayed and discouraged Church. Next, there is the distinct testimony of all the early disciples, without exception, to the fact that this event was nothing else than the resurrection of Jesus Christ from the dead. And lastly, there is no other competing story about the matter which is worthy of a moment's consideration. Christendom and its institutions are explained, and can only be explained, on the hypothesis of Christ's resurrection. Though ingenuity might, therefore, possibly manage to account for Mediæval England without any reference to the battle of Hastings, or some incredible dislike to volcanic catastrophes might attempt to describe the present condition of Pompeii without any allusion to the famous eruption of Vesuvius, yet a far more difficult task lies before the historian who should undertake to account for the existence of the Christian Church only by the shame and defeat of the

Cross, without any mention of the reassuring victory of the Resurrection. Nor could any one give a rational estimate of the character and writings of St. Paul if he proceeded on the supposition that both the great Apostle himself, and Peter and James and John,[1] whom he visited and consulted, were victims to some incurable illusion in their firm persuasion that they had seen and conversed with Jesus after His death.

But if the Resurrection of Christ really took place, then its singular and totally unexpected phenomena present us with a clue towards conceiving what human "immortality" means. It preserves our hope of that result from evaporating into a mere belief in ghosts. And it acquits our doctrine from the charge, which might otherwise be aimed against it by votaries of physical science, that it fails to maintain a connection with the material, tangible and conceivable universe.

Thus the alleged Resurrection of Christ presents itself as a crucial test to every department of our mental being. To our INTELLECT it becomes a test of candour. It puts the question—"Will you firmly shut your eyes to a new phenomenon, supported by considerable proof, simply because at present it fits in with no orthodox biological theory?" To our IMAGINA-

---

[1] *Galatians* i. 18; ii. 9.

TION it appeals with the question—"Will you obstinately prefer to picture men dying like dogs, or passing to an Orcus full of squeaking gibbering shades, or transmigrating through the bodies of beasts, or sinking into a Nirwana-sleep only comparable to the death-life of a batrachian inclosed in a stone, or becoming an occult ghost rapping out doggrel verses beneath a table? Or will you rather welcome a Resurrection-scene of victorious energy and triumphant life, that seems expressly meant to lend itself to artistic treatment and so to become a veritable 'gospel to the poor,' who can follow a dramatic representation, and can easily grasp what is capable of being pictured, though they may not perhaps be able to read or to follow a Platonic argument"? And lastly to the CONSCIENCE, too, this majestic event becomes a test. It seems to say, "Will you—can you possibly—believe that all men, finally and equally, pass into annihilation? Can you hold that a Stephen or a Paul—'most miserable of all men'—are derided and cheated of their hope; while the murderer, the tyrant, the seducer, the swindler, enjoy all that they can desire? Is it possible to conceive that Gavroche, who enjoys Paris down to the very dregs, has reason on his side;[1]

[1] Yet this seems to be M. Renan's, somewhat ironical, conclusion. See an amusing passage in the *Souvenirs*, 9th

while the pale student, who sacrifices his life for the truth, is a fool for his pains, and, with the wreath of steam that has done its work, is tossed away by the wind uncared for and unthanked ? Or will you—calling to mind that not even this wind-tossed vapour itself, nor the force it represents, are really annihilated, though for a time they may disappear—hold fast the conviction that human life, too, does not really perish; and gladly welcome the strong aid to moral stability which Christ's resurrection is calculated to supply?"

In what way these questions will be entertained and answered by each man depends on the quality of his character; and thereby, no doubt, the secret "thoughts of many hearts" are every day revealed. Nor, in view of that result, does the enigma any longer remain obscure why Christ's resurrection was not made a public and overpowering and incontrovertible event, excluding every possibility of doubt or denial; but was rather reserved as a help for those that would be helped, and kept back as an evidence for eyes already couched from materialistic film and dimly

---

Edition, p. 155. "Gavroche [the typical Paris gamin] et M. Homais [the atheistic clockmaker] arrivant d'emblée, et avec si peu de peine, au dernier mot de la philosophie! C'est bien dur à penser."

aware of spiritual verities unseen by organs of sense. For it thus became—as every aid to moral beings necessarily is—a moral, rather than a logical, influence.[1] As a mere "evidence" its force is purposely lowered—as the clearness of our Lord's teaching was purposely lowered by being couched in parabolic forms. But it thereby comes to pass that no man's freedom is invaded and no man's will coerced. Rather a mute appeal, as it were, is made to already receptive souls, "Will ye also go away?" And, by a kind of natural selection, those only are touched and captivated by this great event who are prepared to admit its influence upon their lives.

(3.) The last point of view from which we undertook to approach this difficult subject of

---

[1] "The one point on which the Gospels are agreed in insisting is that our Lord, after rising from the dead, claimed absolute power in heaven and in earth.... In view of this great fact that the Lord was actually living, and that they were in communion with Him, the details of the occurrences which attended His resurrection were of secondary importance."—(Wace, *The Gospel and its Witnesses*, 1883, p. 160.) "The truth of the miraculous credentials of Christianity rests upon various arguments.... Nor in judging upon the force and weight of these arguments can we dispense with the proper state of the affections."—(Mozley, *On Miracles*, p. 235.) "Dieu donne la sagesse à ceux qui se conduisent avec piété, a dit un homme [Wm. of Poitiers, A.D. 1050] habile dans la connaissance des choses divines."—(Guizot, *Mémoires pour servir*, &c., vi., 387.) "C'est par l'âme, avant tout, par la foi, que Jésus veut être connu."—(Bersier, *Sermons*, i., 309.)

LECT. VII.

immortality, was that which is of interest to busy and practical people—viz. from the side of its popular *presentment* in literature and art. Indeed, it is from this quarter, probably, that the deepest repugnance to the doctrine usually takes its rise—impatient scorn being often expressed for conceptions of a future life that seem to pass all bounds of childishness and unreason.[1] Nor can it be honestly said that such scorn is always without excuse. Professor Tyndall is certainly here within his rights when he says:—" Theologians must liberate and refine their conceptions; or must be prepared for the rejection of them by thoughtful minds." [2] And in this conviction he is supported, not only by thousands of English Churchmen, but by able Scottish divines [3] and by French Presby-

---

[1] "I, for my part, have no objection to extinction. I see the old notions of death and of scenes to follow to be so merely human, so impossible to be true, that I see nothing to be done but to wait, without fear or hope."—(Miss Martineau, *Life*, iii., 454.)

[2] Prof. Tyndall, in *Nineteenth Century*, November, 1878; p. 831. Cf. Flügge, *der Himmel*, p. 306.—"Assuredly the Christian belief in a future state is capable of, and urgently needs, elevation, if it is to be regarded as anything more than a popular mythus, and to possess any interest or attraction for cultivated men."

[3] See a collection of "Scotch Sermons," published a few years ago. *E.g.* (1) Caird on *Corporate Immortality*, p. 16:—"The aim of Christian endeavour is, not to look away to an inconceivable heaven beyond the skies, but to realise the latent heaven which human nature and human society con-

terians like the eloquent and pious M. Bersier. This great preacher laments that "the most serious Frenchmen nowadays refuse even to speak of eternity, while many deny a future life with a sort of passion." At the funeral of M. St. Beuve, he says, the service of consolation was reduced to twenty words: "Messieurs! you, who have rendered this last homage to the memory of the dead, be thanked in his name! The ceremony is terminated."[1] And at the funeral of Mr. Darwin in Westminster Abbey, a French *savant* was heard to remark, "Had this event occurred in France, either no priest would have ministered here, or, if he did, no man of science would be present."

Now why is all this? May it not be because Christianity has too much forgotten its freedom, and has allowed itself to be too dependent in this matter upon the Apocalypse? Yet every one nowadays is aware that this Book is poetry, and

---

tain."—(2) Semple, on *Eternal Life*, p. 333:—"Our ideas are drawn chiefly from the Apocalypse; but when once we understand that Eternal Life is a property only of the soul, these splendid descriptions cease to be literal." (3) Stevenson on *Eternal Life*, p. 369:—"Gates of pearl and streets of gold! He who once realises the gulf which separates spiritual life from spiritual death, would refuse them, if they were to risk his spiritual likeness to God." (4) Story, on *Christ's Authority*, p. 376:—"Through demanding that too much be believed, one may induce repugnance to belief altogether."

[1] Bersier, *Sermons*, iv., pp. 216, 188.

poetry of the very deepest Hebrew dye. Every one knows that the "gates of pearl and streets of gold" are metaphors, and is sure that St. Augustine's glorious Gentile "City of God" could be ill confined within the jasper wall of a four-square city, 12,000 furlongs every way, "the length and the breadth and the *height* of it being equal."[1] But still the charm of the Apocalypse, and of books founded on the Apocalypse, is so great that we are almost always tempted to confine our thoughts to its guidance, and forget that, as Dante built up with Mediæval materials his marvellous fancies about the unseen world, and as Milton and Bunyan built with Reformation materials, so we, too, have liberty to build with Modern materials, and are free to quarry (as it were) from the bosom of the soil of our own native land a home for our thoughts to dwell in. Suppose, then, we are, in these days, instructed mainly by Nature; then, from *Nature* and the natural sciences we may allowably derive our modes of thinking about the Future Life. We may reflect, with delight and with profit, how the forces that play amid the universe are (to all appearance) coœval with its existence. We may observe how they suffer transformation, yet are never destroyed; and though latent in coal-seams

---

[1] *Revelation* xxi. 16.

and elsewhere for untold centuries, are suspended, never annihilated. We may repeople past worlds with their strange inhabitants, and know that (in view of them) even our present terrestrial scene is already "a new heavens and a new earth." We may remember the astonishing fact that, looking down the interminable vista of the past, our own life has (virtually) been eternal. For the chain of linked vitality can never once (for millions of years) have been snapped, or we should not be here to-day; so surely has cell passed on to cell its mysterious torch of vitality, since "life" (all science thus far agrees) can never start from the ground afresh; it has always been engendered by some previous life. And then we may reflect how varied are the ways of Nature even in her methods of propagation; so that, as Büchner says, mere customary things deceive us; and the truth is that in the animated world at large an infinite majority of beings know absolutely nothing of either sex or birth.[1]

And so, at last, we come back to the thoughts which inspired the teeming mind of the great Apostle, St. Paul. For what is it that he really says in that noble chapter to the Corinthians which deals with the Church's "sure and certain hope" of a future life?[2] Is it not this?

[1] *Vie et Lumière*, p. 258.
[2] The soberness of the Church's official language on this

LECT. VII.

"The resurrection of Jesus Christ gives the clue to all our thoughts. In Adam—that is, in the physical manhood we received by generation—we die: in Christ—that is, in the spiritual manhood of *re*-generation—we live. And observe that law and order reign even here. Christ is the first fruits; and then by degrees the kingdom of life permeates everywhere. But for this hope, why fight with beasts at Ephesus and 'die daily,' and why such reverential care for dead friends, that some even dream of vicarious rituals for them? Rather let us embrace pessimism. Let us make believe we are beasts, and eat and drink like them, for to-morrow, like them, we are to be annihilated! But a man may ask, how are the dead raised, and with what *body* do they come? O vain and foolish and anxious curiosity! Canst thou not leave that problem in the hands of God? *Only think of His amazing wealth of forms as displayed in Nature.*[1] Think of celestial bodies and terres-

---

subject is very remarkable. It never pretends to rise above the level of faith and hope. For "the hope of continuance after our death can never be more than an act of faith: demonstrated science it can never be."—(Flügge, *Der Himmel*, p. 326.)

[1] "A single drop of water," says Prof. Owen, "may contain 500,000,000 infusoria, whose difference of size is greater than that between a mouse and an elephant."—(Somerville, *Physical Geography*, ii., 67.) "Nearly 40,000 species of plants and animals have been added to the Linnæan-list by palæontological research."—(Huxley, *Lay Sermons*, p. 224.) Yet,

trial bodies, of birds and fishes, beasts and men! Why the very stars at white heat, or yellow, or red, or dull, differ from one another in radiance.[1] *If God will that thou shalt live again, never fear but that from His rich storehouse some frame, most suitable to thy new environment, shall be forthcoming for thy clothing.* But personal *continuity* —how about that? Well: is not the seed, whose rude, unsightly form is dissolved and lost in the furrow, continuous with the lovely waving miracle of beauty that stands erect there in the summer days of harvest? Is it lost because (in a sense) it died? Has it vanished because no one would know it again? Is it annihilated because its old *shape* has disappeared, and God—from select and prepared material, nursed in ovary after ovary of the past, and living on with an eternal vitality when the ancillary stalk and root and leaf and husk are rejected and gone—has built up at last this lovely thing, full of energy, grace, and utility? Even so, we shall not all sleep, but we shall be changed, and death shall be swallowed up in victory."

"from man himself down to the lowest fungus or alga, every organism begins with a minute spheroidal mass of protoplasm. And all animals and plants never fail to be resolvable into oxygen, hydrogen, nitrogen, and carbon."—(Mivart, in *Contemporary Review*, July, 1879, p. 696.)

[1] Cf. Büchner, *Lumière*, &c., p. 72.

LECT. VII.

I confess I do not see, with all the newest lights that science has cast upon the world of matter—for science cannot go one step beyond that—how St. Paul's glowing and yet reserved language could well be improved upon. No one really knows what "life" is; and therefore no one really knows what "death" is.[1] Though it be the commonest of all phenomena, yet science has not one word to say about life; but only about matter when life is absent from it; or chemistry, perhaps, is busy remodelling the architecture which life had built up. *Sleep*, too, "twin-brother of death,"[2] is totally unexplained. *Generation* is more mysterious and inexplicable even than death. Assimilation of *food* is a daily resurrection of dead matter. *Repair*, by choice and direction of material—as the great blood-river goes rushing by, and each organ dips for the stuff it wants—is so far beyond all imagination, that the growth of a finger-nail is an incomprehensible miracle. *Cell-life* and amœba-life—10,000 separate lives within our veins, yet all subordinate and incorporate in the one life that rules and acts and thinks for all—there is a "mystery" we all carry about with us every day.[3]

---

[1] See Bishop Butler, *Analogy*, part i., chap. i.
[2] *Iliad*, xiv. 231.
[3] Dr. Caton, of Liverpool, has observed even a migration of these white amœba-like corpuscles in the blood through the

And thus, amid our idle play and still idler business, we are to ourselves a standing parable and daily type of that higher truth which we find it so hard to believe [1]—*the ultimate Victory of Life*

---

walls of the arteries, while no red corpuscles ever act in tha way.—(See *Academy*, February 1, 1871.)

[1] No Christian teacher, worthy of the name, will ever deny that the doctrine of Immortality—even when confirmed by that most merciful aid to our faith, the visible conquest of death by Jesus Christ—is a very difficult and inconceivable doctrine. But its difficulty is immensely increased by official recognition of crude popular conceptions, as if they were themselves matters *de fide*. Their crudity, of course, is perpetually liable to exposure. For instance, Sir John Herschel, in the *Fortnightly Review* (June 3, 1865), pointed out the following facts: That at the end of only 3,000 years the human race, if replaced upon this globe, would number 460,000 millions, and would be piled up, body upon body, to 3,674 times the height of the sun from the earth. Hence people who confound popular notions with essential Christian truth often feel, with Miss Martineau, overpowered by the difficulties of such notions, and their faith and hope (quite unnecessarily) give way. That lady's account of her own feelings in immediate prospect of death is most sad and most touching. She says: "I find death the simplest thing in the world, a thing not to be feared or regretted, or to get excited about in any way. The dying naturally and regularly desire, and sink into, death as into sleep. Rest is all they think about."—(*Autobiography*, ii. 435.) But add to such restful feelings the Christian's quiet "hope" of immortality and loving "desire to be with Christ," and then death may be blessed and peaceful indeed. Nor do we doubt that "Ceux qui ont persévéré, qui ont cru, qui ont espéré contre toute espérance, ont fini par avoir raison."—(Montalembert, *Avenir d'Angleterre*, p. 280.) "The belief in a future life has strengthened many hands, ennobled many lives, comforted many thousands of the afflicted. It is a beautiful creed, the most

LECT. VII.

over *Death*, the construction out of that "which every joint supplieth" of the Spiritual Body of Christ, and the shaping and harmonising of myriads of "living stones" into a social structure (cemented by a divine love), Christ Himself being the chief corner-stone—"in whom all the building, fitly framed together, groweth unto an holy Temple in the Lord, builded together for an habitation of God through the Spirit."[1]

beautiful, in its purified form, that humanity has yet created.'—(*Westminster Review*, October, 1883, p. 430.)

[1] "Universum humanum genus est sicut unum corpus ex diversis membris constitutum."—(Pomponatius, 1534, *De Immortalitate Animæ*, p. 5.)

LECTURE VIII.

CONCLUSION.

St. John v. 68 :—"Then said Jesus unto the twelve, 'Will ye also go away?' Peter answered Him, 'Lord, to whom shall we go? Thou hast the words of eternal life.'"

IN this most touching scene, which followed and terminated a day of great perplexity and controversy at Capernaum, we have (I think) an almost exact picture of the state of mind which is prevalent in England at the present moment. We have passed through a half-century of grave perplexity, and of controversy reaching down to the very bases of our most cherished beliefs. We have seen and heard —nay, we have many of us felt to the innermost core of our being—doubt assailing the fundamental truths by which our fathers and mothers, and we ourselves as children, lived. Coming in like an inexorable tide, wave after wave of fresh discovery drove us from our childish sand-castles of Biblical theology, by which we pleased ourselves and thought we "knew something as we ought to know." Until at last, abandoning our crude speculations on the meaning of prophecy and the bearings of the Apocalypse, and foregoing our puerile notions about a divine Mechanic who constructed and occasionally repaired for man's use the great engine of the universe, we were driven back to the foot of towering cliffs (as it were) of perplexity that seemed absolutely insurmountable. We stood, with Mr. Herbert Spencer, in face of the Unknowable. But some of us, even in that last dread resort, still "in patience possessed our souls." We found that the greatest saints and doctors of the Church, and the inspired prophets of the Bible, with one voice acknowledged that the ultimate problems of theology are inscrutable —in short, that "no man hath seen God at any time." And then we heard the Master's voice— clear and still amid all the inrushing waves of perplexity—"O ye of little faith! Wherefore did ye doubt?"

Such faith, "little" though it may be, is never without its reward. For it grows, and at length it removes mountains; simply because it is, as Jesus said, a "mustard-seed" that has life, and not a pebble without life. It is the strife, through which we attain a settled and established peace. It is the burden and heat of the day, which nobly borne leads on to a tranquil thankful eventide and to a glowing sunset which "repeats the glory of its prime." Nay, how tenfold more glorious, better, grander, happier, is the gray-haired man or woman who has retained—or re-attained—the heart of child-like simplicity than even that most lovely thing the world contains, the joyous innocent child! And so it is in spiritual life. He that endureth, that believeth, that hopeth in spite of all appearances—that has a faith of Abraham and calmly walks through every seeming impossibility, a faith of St. Paul that "only they are crowned and sainted who with grief have been acquainted," a faith taught by Christ Himself that through apparent defeat and death lies the way to a victorious resurrection of energy and life —only such a person (I say) finds out at last how "faithful is He that hath promised," and discovers that "blessed is the man who endureth temptation; for when he is tried, he shall receive the crown of life." Indeed in all search after truth, a certain divine gift of patience is required, and a certain peaceableness both towards others and within the hidden realm of one's own conscience. And this atmosphere of peace nothing can so well engender as a steadfast persistency in well-doing, in spite of the seeming immorality of nature around us, and a firm "continuance in prayer"—that is, in a tranquillising routine of divine worship, and in soothing communion with that all-embracing, all-permeating Spirit, who "is not far from any one of us." For that all-harmonising and ruling force has evidently (as Bishop Butler reminds us) appointed to some persons "mental perplexity"[1] as their schooling for higher things and their special life's probation. We may not, therefore, evade that schooling, nor refuse that probation; still less, should we think evil of it or foolishly regard perplexity as wrong in itself. Loyally accepted and thankfully made use of, it may become the highest right and plainest duty. And then, of course, it will not disturb our calm nor destroy our peace.[2] Side-lights will unexpectedly reveal the contour of a subject, if we quietly let the sun go round. Even "unconscious cerebration" (as it is called) often does half the work, if you will let it—as people sometimes

---

[1] Dr. Wigan, *On Insanity*, p. 428.

[2] "How can a man without calm obtain happiness" (says the Hindu Bhagavat-gita). "He who abandons his own interest in the fruit of his actions is always contented and independent."—(Thomson's translation, pp. 19 and 32.)

"Calm yourself," said Jean Paul some fifty years ago. "It is your first necessity. Be a Stoic, if nothing else will serve."
—(Ap. Froude, *Life of Bunyan*, p. 53.)

solve an abandoned problem in their sleep. All things come to them that can wait. "Wait on the Lord, therefore, and keep His way; and He shall make thee to inherit the land"—the promised land, at last, of sweet and calm assurance about all things that are essential, of loving tolerance about all things that remain doubtful, of joyful concurrence with those traditional ways of Christendom which have for eighteen centuries preached the Gospel to the poor and overspread the earth (as nothing else could do) with a vast network of brotherly kindness and charity.

For behold, at this day, what wonders a little "quietness and confidence" have worked! No one, I think, can attentively watch what is going on in England at present without a strong conviction growing upon him that the onset of unbelief (unless something should occur to renovate it) has somewhat exhausted its force. The reasons for this conviction are twofold. First, the negative one, that physical science, which seemed at first so formidable and so likely to organise itself into an anti-Christian shape, has now for a good many years had the opportunity, and has proved itself powerless to achieve anything of the kind. And though the author of *Natural Religion* good-humouredly suggests that the profound awe and admiration of the universe which many "physicians" cherish is, of itself, a sort of religion—a thing which I should be the last to deny—still nothing definite has ever come of these high sentiments. The feeling has engendered no cultus; the mollusk (as it were) has elaborated no chambered shell to dwell in; no temples have arisen; no congregations have assembled. Mankind at large are none the better, nor the worse, for it all. And though for individuals this love of nature is indeed beautiful and elevating, yet socially and religiously it seems impotent and sterile. Two only attempts have been even hazarded in this direction, viz., POSITIVISM for the refined—a mere philosophy, a scheme for idealising Man instead of the Cosmos, in which man forms an infinitesimal part; and SECULARISM for the lower classes, its very name indicating the fact that its heart is set on politics rather than religion, and that it is of this world to the very core. Now it is surely a most remarkable and instructive fact that, amid an atmosphere of unlimited religious liberty, and with buildings facing us in every street for the shelter of emphatically "free churches" and "independent" forms of belief and worship, no worship of Nature should ever yet have been able to get so much as a foothold; and that, with all her splendid successes in the intellectual sphere, *science has morally and religiously* remained to this hour inconstructive. Yet the reason is, perhaps, not far to seek. Intellect, which is the cold steel wherewith science mainly works, is an essentially analytic and not a constructive power. It dissects, it distinguishes, it splits even sunbeams and molecules, it subdivides into ever-growing mazes of bewildering detail its own studies and classifications and theories. But these infinitesimals are not the stuff of which popular "religions" are made. Religions are built of coarser blocks. They are suited to express bold and large generalisations, involving much error and exaggeration. They are purposely constructed—or rather they spontaneously grow without purposed "construction" — to give a shelter to great brotherhoods of man, to embrace varieties of sex and age and education, and so to teach mankind by forcible, intrepid action (what science tries in vain to teach them by the way of delicate and airy speculation) the unity of the world and the solidarity (as the phrase is) of man and of the living beings that the world contains.

"Match me such marvel, save in Eastern clime."

The West has (it seems) grown too prosaic—perhaps too cynical — to engender any more blazing enthusiasms of religious conviction. Arabia (it seems) can still engender such things. But America, for instance, cannot get beyond the extremely comfortable sentimentalism of the "Latter-day Saints."

It appears, therefore, to be the simplest common-sense, as well as the highest loyalty to that Power which guides all the evolutions of the world, to embrace and use and develop to the uttermost the splendid opportunity we have inherited from our forefathers in their bequest of the Christian Church. We Englishmen especially possess an organised Christianity, which has carried us already through twelve centuries of (I venture to say) as magnificent and "sacred" a history as ever belonged to the Greeks, the Romans, or even to the Hebrews themselves. And at this moment, after waiting long in anxious expectation to see what religious ideas the physical sciences would engender, our people are beginning to break the spell of silence, and to demand that their time-honoured Church shall bestir itself to fresh efforts of revival and reform. Indeed, there are symptoms of an almost fanatical impatience. And, in some quarters, even new and untried methods are without scruple invented for bringing Christianity to bear upon mankind. Thus, by one system, the very outcasts and pariahs of society have been brought under some kind of discipline and been taught the first rudiments of obedience and service. By another system thousands of working men and women have been drawn together, and have been swayed, like standing corn, before the breath of their popular preachers. And among the higher classes, in London especially, such a happy deployment of Christian energy and unselfishness is now visible on every hand, that a German writer on Socialism in England has ventured on an inference too good (I fear) to be true. He thinks that "the abyss formerly yawning between our upper and our lower classes has thereby been now virtually bridged over."[1]

But whether this be true or not, any way an assurance is rapidly dawning upon us all *that there is no essential contradiction between science and Christianity*. Such contradictions as still exist are maintained chiefly by ignorance on the one side and by prejudice on the other. They are, in short, little better than the ghosts of once contending armies hovering uselessly about a deserted battle-field. Most of them, indeed, arise from pure misunderstanding. For instance, Dr. Büchner complains that "religion tolerates no doubt, no discussion, no investigation."[2] Yet all Protestants agree that moral faith and intellectual uncertainty are (in some way) correlatives, and that faith

---

[1] Brentano, *English Socialism*, p. 71.
[2] *Man in the Past*, &c., p. 219.

LECT. VIII.

cannot rise to any great height without the simultaneous presence of doubt. Discussion, again, has been the very life and vital breath of the Church, from the beginning till now. And, as to rational investigation, it is actually one of the Apostolic precepts—"Be ready always to give a *reason* for the hope that is in you;"[1] "Add to your faith virtue and to virtue *knowledge*."[2] Nevertheless, Sunday lecturers in London tell us, "The religions say this, or this, is truth which you reject at your peril, and must accept on our authority."[3] Even a woman can lament that "sadness is for the Christian, whose world lies under the curse of an angry God."[4] While an American orator soars thus into the very empyrean of absurdity: "Religion accepts only the homage of the prostrate, and scorns the offerings of those who stand erect. She cannot tolerate the liberty of thought. The wide and sunny fields belong not to her domain. The starlit heights of genius are above and beyond her appreciation and power. Her subjects cringe at her feet, covered with the dust of obedience."[5]

---

[1] 1 Peter, iii. 15. [2] 2 Peter, i. 5.
[3] Dr. Wild, *A Freethinker's Vindication*, 1884, p. 7. Contrast Greg. Gt., *Moralia*, viii. 3. "Ea quæ assero, nequaquam mihi ex auctoritate credite: sed, an vera sint, ex ratione pensate!"   [4] Mrs. Besant, *Gospel of Atheism*, 1882, p. 4.
[5] Ingersoll, *Difficulties of Belief*, p. 10.

I suppose it is quite useless to tell all these people that they are under a gross mistake—that Christianity is exactly the opposite of all that they suppose—that the watchword of St. Paul is, "Stand fast in the liberty wherewith Christ hath made you *free*," and that the first summons of St. Peter to a prostrate convert was, "Stand up; I myself also am a man!" For prejudice builds up as solid a wall to shut out religion, as pious ignorance often builds to exclude science. And if any missile is considered good enough wherewith to assail Christianity, it is always easy to pick up some chance words of anti-Christian bigotry, such as those which M. Renan gathered from his Ultramontane teachers: "Christian belief hangs on the principle of Infallibility: if I relax my hold on any one point, I relax my hold on all."[1] Or as these, which appeared lately even in an English review: "To doubt wilfully any one article of faith, or to enter on the examination of any dogma with the intention of *suspending* belief until the conclusion of such examination, would be for a Catholic a deadly sin."[2] All such statements, however, are already ridiculed by Abelard in the twelfth century. He says, "People assert that

---

[1] *Souvenirs*, p. 301.
[2] Monsignor Capel in *Nineteenth Century*, February, 1880, p. 361.

nothing pertaining to the Catholic faith is to be investigated by reason; but if this were accepted, every false religion would entrench itself against us behind the selfsame plea."[1] At any rate for a Protestant it certainly is not a deadly sin, but a way—a sea-way, if you will—rough with waves, and vexed with veering winds, and taxing to the energy and courage of those that sail thereby. And therefore it is buoyed with warnings of hidden peril and lighted with beacons amid the night of "doubt and sorrow" that comes to so many of us in these days. Nor is it unfurnished with havens of refuge for those who are unequal to the struggle. For confessedly it is not good for *all* to be harassed with doubt; but only for some. And this fact it is which adds such subtle difficulty to the task of Christian pastors and preachers, that they might well (I think) have looked for more sympathy and patience from thoughtful men of science than they have usually found.

But difficult as may be the task of preaching Christ in an age like this, and to congregations composed of the most strangely-mixed ingredients, it is not quite impossible to do so; nor has the simple word of the Gospel ever yet lost its attractive power for any human being, whatever be his

[1] *Introduction to Theology*, lib. ii. p. 1050 (ed. Migne).

stage of thought, who has honestly reviewed his own character, and has seen there, in vivid contrast with each other, the ideal that he might have been and the real that he is. The poignant sense of that terrible contrast is what Christianity means by "sin." And the more, under some system or other—for without "system" of some kind the soul goes to shipwreck and ruin — that grand truth is realised, which both science and Christianity proclaim, viz., the unity, continuity, and superhuman majesty of the universe, the more agonising becomes the conviction that fretful, self-willed, self-degraded man forms the sole and shameful exception, amid a surrounding world of unswerving obedience to divine and glorious Law.[1] The laws of physical nature we cannot help obeying. Yet even them we sometimes, by our blundering and wilful mismanagement, fail to harmonise and direct aright. We clear our forests, till the climate is spoiled: we build sea-walls, till the beach is swept away and our houses tumble down: we try to ward off typhus, and manage to inoculate our food and our homes with its fatal poison: we set up lightning-conductors, and bring the destroying flash down into our public buildings. All these faults are, in a sense, physical "sins." They are illustrations and types of those

[1] See Hooker, *Ecclesiastical Polity*, book i.

far worse moral sins which bring discord and ruin into the conscience. Indeed, the great chemist Liebig falls quite spontaneously into language of this sort. He says, "I could not discover why the effect of my chemicals was so tardy. At last, I discovered the reason: *I had sinned against the wisdom of the Creator*, and suffered just punishment. I had fancied, in my blindness, that the alkalies must be made insoluble, else the rain would carry them off." [1]

But if these things are "sins" and follies, what are we to say to the disobedience which spoils and degrades our own characters; and poisons, with vicious habit and memory of deeds and words beyond recall, our very hearts? Surely there is no one—"scientific" as he may deem himself, and far removed from all superstition and credulity—who positively wants no religious help at all; who needs no redemption; craves no pardon; lacks no peace. There is no one who can boldly waive aside as of no consequence to him (or her) that gracious invitation addressed by Christ to all, "*Come unto ME, and I will give you rest!*"

Thousands, millions, have already come, and have found His promise true. Thousands have been taught—not by the way of microscopes and

---

[1] "Agricultural Chemistry," in *Contemporary Review*, April, 1877, p. 882.

telescopes (for these have often narrowed, while they deepened, the powers of mental vision), but by the shorter way of the heart's surrender—that the dread power which holds all things in unity is willing to re-embrace *them* too in unity, and to bathe their minds in light and peace. And so surrendering themselves to God by Christ, they have awoke to the firm conviction that the universe is neither dead nor dying, nor the spirit that pervades it either a brute instinct or a blind fate—but human (so to speak) and mirrored, "as in a glass, darkly," upon the tranquil surface of their inner man. They have learnt, too, the full meaning of that specially Christian summons, "*Sursum corda!*" Lift up your hearts! In other words, "Take larger views of what that most sacred of all words, 'GOD,' really imports. Kindred to you, and partly intelligible, as this Almighty Power may be, remember that He is quite infinitely super-human and super-personal. And from the fact that your mind and conscience can reflect a few beams only of His universal radiance, learn modesty and hesitation. For your highest knowledge cannot be more than relative and your best conceptions are utterly inadequate. Be thankful, therefore, that your weakness has not been asked for impossibilities, for positive knowledge, for absolute assurance, or for a never-

LECT. VIII.

failing concurrence with God's will; but that easy moral graces, capable of infinite gradations from less to more, viz., Faith, Hope, and Love, have been alone required." Yes: inspired by these, a man may walk the world a different being, "a new creature." He is redeemed from all harassing necessity for clear-cut certainty in religion, and is taught by Christ that a heart's FAITH and trust are quite enough. He is released from tormenting thoughts about the haziness that shrouds the future, being tranquillised by the assurance that HOPE is all which is expected of a Christian. And he learns, on the highest possible authority, a truth to which the ever-growing experience of life gives ample confirmation, that—

> " 'Tis the heart, and not the brain,
> Which the highest doth attain;"[1]

in other words, that improved character — not sharpened intellect—forms the best aid for the solution of the highest problems of all; that LOVE of goodness has a moral insight into heavenly things, such as mere intelligence can never attain; and that our Lord's words to Nicodemus have a meaning which men of high education, above all, should lay to heart:—*It is not by learning a lesson from a teacher, nor by conning*

[1] Longfellow.

a task out of a sacred book, but by a re-birth of character (as it were) into a higher ideal world, that a man can alone enter the bright realm of heavenly serenity and joy. "The good Shepherd," says a bold thinker of the second century, "cares indeed for all His sheep; but He seeks especially for such as are of finest quality and most abundant productiveness: and such are men of power and leading, and persons of highly cultivated minds."[1] And to such men as these, at the present crisis of His Church, He seems almost audibly to appeal: "The selfish and the sensuous have abandoned Me, the idle and the frivolous have gone their way, the worshippers of wealth have despised Me. Of them I expected nothing better. But will ye also go away?"

[1] Clement of Alexandria, *Strom*, vi. 17.

INDEX.

ABELARD, a free-thinker, 12.
Æons, Gnostic notion of, 9.
Animals have no sense of sin, 97.
Anthropomorphism necessary, 33.
—— involves ideas of power, wisdom, goodness, 51.
Apocalypse, poetry of, 158.
Apostles, not victims of illusion, 152.
Assyrian tablets deciphered, 30.

Bacon's *Novum Organum*, 16.
Balaam, story of, 89.
Belief, now rudely shaken, 1.
—— causes of its decline, 4.
Brentano, views of England, 173.
Büchner, nature-worship, 19.
Buddhism, modern attraction towards, 136.

Chance, irrational, 65.
Christianity the salvation of modern society, 126.
—— suitable for all mankind, 140.
Christ a unique character, 93.
—— His spirit has seized the modern world, 86.
Church, bound to be truthful, 74.
—— attracts different types of mankind, viii.
—— inspires respect, vii.
—— modern revival of, 172.
Clement of Alexandria a great thinker, 11.
Clergy should sympathise with liberty, 94.
Controversies, how they arise, 21.
Cosmic force awful, 61.
—— not blind or malignant, 49.
Courage needed nowadays, 6.
Creation, Christian view of, 52.
—— proceeded by stages, 53.
—— the only tenable theory, 67.

Dark ages knew not Nature's Unity, 83.

Darwin, disciples of, 17.
Defences of Christianity need reviewing, 71.
Degradation not irremediable, 123
—— moral, revolt against, 121.
Deity, how conceivable by us, 51
Doubt, modern, 165.
—— a form of probation, 169.

Ecclesiastical art, use of, xi.
England, as viewed by Americans, xv.
—— summoned to high efforts, 69.
—— characteristics of, 7.
Evil, undeniable, 107.
Evolution, does not contradict creation, 56.
—— in harmony with all Christian doctrine, 67.
—— does not explain the origin of evil, 37.

Faculties, limitation of, 141.
Faith, not certainty, 179.
—— essential in all mental operations, 44.
—— never without reward, 166.
—— implies doubt, 174.
—— a common ground, 23.
Fall, the Christian view, 110.
—— Semitic poem of the, 112.
—— compatible with evolution, 105.
Fanaticism and Atheism, 25.
Fate an irrational conception, 59.
Force, transmutations of, 149.
—— different from matter, 41.
Freedom gloried in by St. Paul, x.
Future life shrouded in mystery, 141.
—— and annihilation, 153.
—— and evolution, 152.
—— St. Paul's view of, 160.

Generations have their own duties to fulfil, 5.
Genesis, poetry of, 53.
Geology in the last generation, 31.

Gnosticism grew to be a heresy, 10.
God, inadequate language about, 36
—— not impersonal, 50.
—— not arbitrary, 70.
—— indispensable to most men, 47.
Gravitation, illustration from, 32.

Hartmann scornful about creation, 54.
History sacred to Englishmen, 172.
Humanity, moral failure of, 122.

Ideals, redeeming power of, 131.
Imagination, influence of, 21.
—— the first to awake, 127.
—— makes things human, 29.
Immortality, law of, 144.
Intellect and imagination, 24.
—— restless, 21.
Investigation an Apostolic precept, 174.

John, his Logos doctrine, 9.
Joshua, miracle of, 89.

Knowledge relative, 43.

Liberty given by Ritual, ix.
Life, new forms of, 148.
—— mystery of, 163.
—— unbroken chain of, 159.
—— its victory over Death, 163.
Logos, the Reason of God, 58.

Man, his first appearance, 113.
—— his momentary innocence, 103.
Matter and Force, 41.
Mind and Matter, 53.
Miracles a crucial problem, 69.
—— no violation of Law, 75.
—— engendered belief, 85.
—— not *a priori* impossible, 71.
—— the goal, not the threshold of belief, 91.
—— matter for historical inquiry, 72.
Moleschott, on "necessity," 59.
Monotheism taught through Miracle, 84.

Nature, unity of, 52.
Nursery, a study of human nature, 127.

Pain, physical and moral, 122.
Patience in seeking for truth, 167.
Paul, his westward progress, 8.
—— on the resurrection, 161
Physical science a sort of new revelation, x.
Physical and moral sin, 177.
Positivism, 34.
Prayer, how suggested, 50.

Races, new and old, 147.
Redemption, meaning of, 116.
Reformation, benefit of, 69.
Religion, effects moral change, 125.
—— its work is to idealise, 28.
Restlessness, modern, 137.
Resurrection of Christ, 151.

Salvation, schemes of, 118.
Schopenhauer, 38.
Science should be Christian, 69.
Secularism, political, 170.
Shame, a human characteristic, 96.
Sin, original, 99.
Spencer and the "carpenter-theory," 55.
Strauss confesses beauty of Christ's character, 85.
System needful, of some kind, 177.

Theism rational, 43.
Theological burdens should be lightened, ix.
Tolerance, duty of, 26.
Truth, a paramount object, 73.
Tyndall on the Imagination, 55.

Unbelief recurrent, 21.
Unity, indispensable to man's thought, 169.
—— taught by Genesis, 53.
Unknown, awfulness of the, 166.

Waves of scientific objection, 8.
West, barren of religious enthusiasm, 171.
Will, stimulated by motives, 64.
Wisdom and goodness cannot be unconscious, 49
Women, affected by modern unbelief, 3.
Worship, restful effect of, 168.

www.ingramcontent.com/pod-product-compliance
Lightning Source LLC
Chambersburg PA
CBHW020911230426
43666CB00008B/1412